LIVIN' LEAN

with Trader Joe's®

Lose Weight and Feel Great
Using Trader Joe's® Products

BY JAMIE DAVIDSON, M.S.

This book is dedicated to all of my clients with whom I have had the honor of working. The transformations you have made in your own lives have been nothing short of phenomenal. Thank you for the privilege.

Copyright © 2011 by Jamie Davidson, M.S.

Designed by: Heather Smith, Heatha B Design.
HeathaBDesign@gmail.com

Editors: Dianne Jacob and Cynthia Leslie-Bole
Proofreader: Christina Richards

Printed in the United States of America

ISBN 978-0-9667309-5-1

This book is not affiliated with nor sponsored by Trader Joe's Company. Trader Joe's is a registered trademark of Trader Joe's Company.

Products featured in this cookbook may only be available in Trader Joe's locations on the West Coast.

Trader Joe's changes its products often. Products used in the cookbook may or not be available. Check online at www.HealthyTraderJoes.com for product updates.

You can find the location of your nearest Trader Joe's by looking on its website: www.traderjoes.com under "locations".

Also by Jamie Davidson

Quick and Healthy Meals using Trader Joe's Products
Simmering Solutions, Healthy Slow-Cooker Recipes
Quick and Healthy Meals from Trader Joe's

Table of Contents:

Introduction

I received an email last year that brought tears to my eyes. A woman wrote that she had lost over 70 pounds and had found my *Quick and Healthy Meals from Trader Joe's* cookbook essential in her efforts to lose weight. One of the reasons she was overweight was that she didn't know how to cook and had been eating excess calories from restaurant and take-out food. My book helped her put together simple yet flavorful meals with ease, and learning these new skills gave her the confidence to make the healthy meals that helped her lose weight. I thought to myself, if a cookbook without any of the other information I give to my weight-loss clients can help bring about that much change, what would the impact be of a cookbook that includes my "What Works Weight Loss™" program? It dawned on me that such a book would be more than a cookbook; it would be a one-stop guide to help those who want to lose weight and improve their health while still managing a busy life.

Of all the hats I wear professionally, coaching clients who want to make changes in their lifestyle to become slimmer, stronger and healthier is the one I am most passionate about. The journey my clients undertake requires courage and perseverance. The physical and emotional transformation they experience often seems nothing short of magical. I am deeply honored to be part of their journey as my clients achieve their goals and create the body and life they want. My hope is that this book will support my clients, as well as people I've never worked with directly, in this exciting journey.

When I teach my weight management classes or work privately with clients, people are always curious to know how I became an expert in weight management. They want to know if I can truly relate to their struggles to lose weight. I assure them that I have walked in their shoes, having been 40 pounds over my current weight at one time. I also assure them that I work at staying slim every day. I use the habits, tools, behaviors, tips and recipes you will find in this book.

In addition to my personal weight loss experience, I have a Master's degree in Exercise Physiology focusing on the effects of exercise on weight loss. I was the fitness director at a YMCA, helping numerous clients get into shape or better shape. I also directed a cardiac rehabilitation program at a hospital.

My focus in this position was helping patients make profound lifestyle changes so they could continue to experience this wondrous gift called "life". Working with these inspiring, courageous patients made a huge impact on my commitment to eating well and exercising and to helping others do the same.

While directing the cardiac rehabilitation program, I designed and directed a weight management program where patients made life-changing alterations to how and what they ate and how much they moved. I also trained and worked as a behaviorist with a medical fasting program for patients who had large amounts of weight to lose and keep off.

Since then, I have been teaching wellness programs to corporations as well as working with private individuals, one-on-one and in groups. I offer cooking classes that teach busy people how to eat well conveniently with my "Quick and Healthy Meals from Costco and Trader Joe's" classes. I also offer numerous other wellness-based classes and programs, including those on how to prepare two weeks of healthy meals in one day, how to feed children well, and how to lose weight with my What Works Weight Loss™ program.

In addition to my teaching, several years ago I began coaching individuals and small groups who wanted personalized weight management coaching. I have found this customized coaching to be rewarding and heartwarming because I am able to help my clients learn what works for their individual lifestyles and experience the success they have been seeking.

As you will see, the recipes in this cookbook come from a wide variety of sources. Some are my own creations, and others come from my cooking class participants, clients, and friends. Some are adaptations of recipes from other cookbook authors and bloggers. All have been tested, sometimes numerous times, to ensure that the recipe works perfectly the first time.

My hope is that this book's easy recipes, menus, shopping lists, snack ideas, suggested accompaniments to entrées and other practical tools and information will enable you to choose and prepare the foods that will help you to get fit and trim and stay that way. I would love to hear about your progress. Please email me at Jamie@HealthyTraderJoes.com or Jamie@WhatWorksWeightLoss.com.

Chapter 1:

I Know How to Lose Weight. How Come I Just Can't Do It?

Every single client with whom I have worked has asked that question within the first five minutes of our conversation. Most have been on and off every diet imaginable for years and are frustrated and embarrassed that, despite being so accomplished in so many areas of their lives, having a trim or even normal-weighted body eludes them. You may be able to relate.

Upon further investigation into what and how much these clients eat, as well as their activity level, it becomes apparent why they have not been successful in the long run. Many who go on a weight loss plan hope that when they have lost their excess weight, they will be able to ease up on the effort it took to lose the weight. But most people gain back the weight they have lost when they ease up, and sadly, some gain even more, despite their good intentions to keep those extra pounds off.

I often tell my clients that eating as a slender person is a learned behavior, just as is eating as a larger person. We learn to eat from those around us just like we

learn other behaviors such as brushing our teeth twice a day or answering the phone politely. If our parents overate or rewarded us for cleaning our plates, we learned to do that; if we were offered a dessert or something special to eat when we were sad or disappointed, we learn to go to food when we have upsetting events in our lives. One of my favorite examples of learned behavior involving food was from one of my clients. Her young grandson hurt his head and she offered him a popsicle in order to help him feel better. He immediately put it on his head! He obviously had learned to put ice on "boo-boos".

Most of us who have had difficulty with excess weight never learned as children how to monitor ourselves around food. This is something we can learn to do as adults, however, so that we will eat appropriately (when we are hungry) and not use food for whatever emotional reason we may have learned in childhood. We can relearn how to eat in order to have the body size (or nearer to the body size) we desire. We begin by first looking at our current behaviors around food and activity, and we slowly make specific, doable changes that enable us to move toward success.

Clients often tell me that they don't want to obsess about what they are eating or how much exercise they need to do; they say it's too much work. I ask them how much they are currently obsessing about how poorly their clothes fit, how self-conscious they are about how they look, and how their extra weight affects their health. With this new perspective, they often realize that they can choose to use their energy more positively by investing it in their long-term well being.

One of the first things I want to know about a potential client is how motivated she is to lose weight. The behavioral, mental and psychological changes it takes to lose weight and keep it off are multiple and complex. It takes desire, intent and a lot of persistence. You have to really want to be smaller to put in the time, effort and work it takes to be successful. If the potential client believes that there is a magic pill, she is still invested in the false promises of the misleading, multi-billion dollar weight loss industry ads. She is not ready.

I hope that you, however, are ready to begin a successful weight loss program using convenient Trader Joe's products to make simple, fast, and healthy meals. This book will help you succeed. You won't see the word "diet" in this book, however, because when people go on a "diet", they eventually go off a "diet". If you have ever been on a prescribed food plan that was unfamiliar, lacking flavor, or felt deprivational, the likely result was that you probably went back to your old way of eating and moving, which very likely contributed to your being overweight. With this book as a guide, you will be learning how to eat well for the rest of your life, not just to "lose the weight."

How to Take Weight Off and Keep it Off

Realizing that it is far more helpful to emulate those who have been successful with losing and maintaining their weight losses than to go on a "diet", Dr. Doreen Hamilton, a colleague and friend, formally studied our former hospital-based weight management clients who had lost weight and kept it off. She found that those who had done so practiced the following behaviors or practices:

1. Exercise regularly. It's not enough to reduce calories. People who move several times a week are much more likely to lose weight and keep their excess weight off. It doesn't matter whether you walk, skate, run, bike, hike or dance. The point is to make it an activity you enjoy, so you will continue to do it. Add strength training twice a week or more and you will have even more success. Doing so builds more muscle. The more muscle you have, the more calories you burn, even when you are just standing around.

2. Focus on successes. When I meet with clients for follow-up appointments, the first thing I want to know is what they did well that previous week. Did they only eat half of whatever it was they had trouble resisting? Did they get out and walk three times, as they had committed? Did they only have one glass of wine, as opposed to their usual two glasses when out for dinner? When we focus on the positive behaviors, the negative choices lose their power to throw us off course or send us into binge or overeating behavior.

3. Plan ahead and make it convenient to be successful. I wouldn't think of getting in my car and driving 30 miles without checking to make sure there is enough gas. Likewise, if I know I am going to be out for a few hours and won't be stopping for a meal, I take a snack so that I don't come home ravenous and then eat too much (a very common practice among those who are overweight). I make sure that the healthy food I want to eat is in my refrigerator or cupboard. I also make sure the restaurants I go to serve a healthy cuisine so that I can consistently make the good food choices that contribute to staying slim.

Despite having good food and exercise options available, many still continue to make choices that are not conducive to losing weight, often from being physically or emotionally cued to eat by their environment, even when they aren't hungry. As an example, one of my clients worked in an office with a lunchroom that always had high-caloric goodies available.

When she walked into the lunch room to get her lunch from the refrigerator, she was cued to eat the goodie because she saw others enjoying it. She often rationalized that it couldn't have more than a hundred calories for a little piece and then would proceed to eat a little piece plus more, resulting in her eating an extra 200 to 300 calories per day. To avoid being cued to eat in that situation, she decided to bring her lunch in a cooler to keep in her office or car and avoided the lunchroom, thus reducing her caloric intake by 200 to 300 calories per day and enabling her to eventually lose the 15 extra pounds she had been carrying. We all have food cues (some conscious and others unconscious), and when we become aware of theses cues, we can make better choices about what we will eat and how we will exercise, as well as setting up our environments so that we will be successful.

My hope is that you will find this book an invaluable guide in helping you plan what you will eat. Trader Joe's is a great place to find foods that are convenient and easy to prepare. In this cookbook, you will find recipes, product lists and tips to make it easier for you to eat the way you'd like to, despite perhaps not having much time. Suggestions and recipes will make it convenient for you to bring your lunch to work and avoid extra calories at restaurants, cafeterias, vending machines and breakrooms. Two sample weekly menus and grocery lists (with more online at my website: www.HealthyTraderJoes.com) will help you plan your meals and leave the impulse items on the store shelves.

4. Keep food records. Many studies have shown that those who keep food records, whether on paper or online, lose significantly more weight (twice as much) than those who don't. Keeping records allows you to budget your food and liquid calories, analyze when and where you are most likely to overeat or drink, notice when it is easy for you to stay within your caloric goals, see if you are meeting your body's nutritional needs, and track your exercise.

People underestimate how much they eat and overestimate how much activity they are doing. I often tell my clients that I could shop at a discount clothing store for a couple of hours, ignore the price tags, and still have money left in my account after I exit the check-out stand, but that I might become overdrawn if I were to do the same at an exclusive retail clothing store. When we eat without being aware of the "cost", or "price tag," we shouldn't be too surprised that we often eat many more calories than we imagined. Many of those who are heavier than they want to be are not aware of the caloric (as well as fat, sodium, etc.) cost of the food they are consuming, and it often comes as a shock, for example, to learn that a Big Mac and medium fries will cost them 1040 calories and 54 grams of fat. Fortunately, larger chain restaurants now have the caloric and nutritional value of each item on the menu so that we can make our choices with awareness of those values.

Several excellent online tracking systems will help you record your food intake, exercise activity levels and much more. Think of the tracking system as a budget for calories and other nutritional goals. All of the ones listed below are currently free:

- Sparkpeople.com
- Loseit.com
- Livestrong.com
- Caloriecount.com
- FitDay.com
- Fitwatch.com

I am most familiar with Sparkpeople.com. I like the feature that allows you to add your own foods to your database. I suggest that you enter the basic nutritional analysis for the recipes you like from this cookbook under "Add a food." Then go to "Enter a food not listed" and "Save the food," and the recipe will become part of your database listed under "Favorites". The database can help you plan your menus by entering the food and then checking to see if your choices will contribute to your nutrition goals. It will also help you analyze and problem-solve if you see that you need to eat more protein, less salt, or make other adjustments. Sparkpeople.com will also help you keep track of the calories burned while exercising.

Many hand-held food tracking applications make keeping food and exercise records very convenient. Free applications of Sparkpeople.com are available for web-enabled cell phones. A good website describing many other options is www.freedieting.com.

Some websites give the nutritional analysis of many Trader Joe's foods, in case you don't save packages or want to see what would be a good addition to your menu. The ones I am most familiar with are www.livestrong. com and www.fatsecret.com.

5. Nurture yourself regularly with something other than food. You might look to food when you want to feel better, whether emotionally or physically. You may be someone who takes care of everyone else around you, feels stressed and drained, and then eats to take care of yourself. Developing other ways to feel nurtured, comforted, pampered, less stressed and more grounded can help you consume less calories.

Many of my clients are accommodators and put the needs of others before their own. Those who learn to put their needs and wishes on at least the same level as those around them have an easier time making sure there is appropriate food in the house for themselves as well as making time to exercise, choosing activities that nurture them, and choosing restaurants with healthy options.

6. Confront hurtful behavior and set practical, specific, doable goals. You might be in a pattern of perceiving some of your behaviors around food and exercise as "bad" by old diet mentality standards, such as eating a dessert or not getting to the gym as you had fully intended. Many formal diets prescribe a strict protocol to assure weight loss success. If you aren't

able to follow such a strict program, you might blame yourself, thinking you are weak or unmotivated when you find the diet difficult to follow. Thinking that you have failed, yet again, can be a set-up for overeating or binge behavior.

Instead of blaming yourself, it can be helpful to face the unhelpful behavior and set reasonable, doable and specific goals to address the problem area. For example, many of my clients come home in the evening before dinner ravenous and then find that they overeat either while they are preparing dinner or while eating dinner. An example of setting a specific and doable goal is to eat a snack with some protein an hour or two before arriving home. That way you can approach dinner with reasonable hunger and avoid overeating. When you can follow through on your specific doable goals, you experience more success and are motivated to continue.

7. Take setbacks in stride. Stuff happens. Instead of dwelling on what you can't control, take stock of the damage and make plans to move forward. People in the study who did not over-react to setbacks ate less as a result.

8. Get help when you need it. Many of us are "do-it-yourselfers" and feel that we shouldn't need help with something that we deem "should" be so simple. However, if despite knowing how to lose weight you are having trouble doing it, you might find more success if you are accountable to someone who will help you design a reasonable plan and stick with it. Don't underestimate the value of accountability, especially when you are first learning and practicing a new eating or exercise behavior. Some forms of accountability available to you could be a weight-management coach, a trainer at the gym, an online community, a weight loss program or your doctor. It's a good idea to leave family members out of this role as they can hesitate to hold you accountable, or they may have reasons (usually subconscious) for why they don't want you to change.

9. Don't give up. Giving up is easy to do, especially when you aren't seeing the success you feel you deserve after all of your effort. (Make sure you have realistic expectations. If you lose one percent of your body weight per week, you are doing a great job.) Sometimes, it isn't clear why you're not losing weight, despite your best efforts. Sometimes it takes more investigation or changing behaviors or food choices to discern what will work. Sometimes you just have to continue with good eating and exercise behaviors for a while before you see the results you want, despite the ads that say you can lose 10 pounds in a week.

What Else Affects Weight Loss?

Many people have tried to lose weight by lowering their calories and increasing their amount of exercise and yet success has eluded them. Other factors that can influence weight loss include: lack of proper sleep; food allergies or sensitivities; hormones including those involving blood sugar and insulin, appetite regulation, and metabolism; and genetic factors.

Two of the literally hundreds of hormones and neuropeptides (chemical signals that transmit information) involved in regulating weight and weight related-behaviors like hunger, satiety and overeating are ghrelin and leptin. Ghrelin is produced in the gastrointestinal tract and stimulates appetite. Leptin is produced in fat cells and sends a signal to the brain that the body has enough energy stores such as body fat. Many obese people don't respond to leptin's signals even though they have higher levels of leptin, so their brains don't know they are full and they keep on eating.

When you don't get enough sleep, it drives leptin levels down. You won't feel as satisfied after you eat. Lack of sleep also causes ghrelin levels to rise, which means your appetite becomes stimulated. The effects of these two - not feeling satiated and having an increased appetite could set the stage for overeating.

Hormonal fluctuations coinciding with menopause can also change the way your body uses calories. For comprehensive information on hormones and menopause, read Dr. Christiane Northrup's book, *The Wisdom of Menopause* or visit her website at www.drnorthrup.com.

A physical workup by a physician may help determine if the above issues are interfering with weight loss. A good eating plan and moderate exercise program can often help regulate many of the functions involved in your body's ability to lose weight.

How to Get Movement into Your Day

If you work at a desk or sit for most of the day, it can be difficult to get enough movement and activity into your day. To lose weight and keep it off, you must engage in some sort of activity on a regular basis. You may say you don't have time to exercise, but research shows that even 10 minutes of exercise, three times a day, benefits overall health. To gain the benefits of being aerobically fit, you need to exercise aerobically for at least 20 minutes three non-consecutive days a week. Exercise that builds muscle such as strength training is also important. As we age, having strong muscles helps prevent osteoporosis and helps us burn more calories.

For more information about target heart rate and the benefits of being aerobically fit, go to my website: www.HealthyTraderJoes.com.

Many of my clients start out as non-movers. I have found that that most people are willing to exercise if they figure out how to make it:

1. Convenient.
2. Enjoyable. You don't have to like it in the beginning, but if it's something you enjoy, you're more likely to keep it up.

3. Engaging. Take a class, walk or play tennis with a friend or join a fundraising group walking for a worthy cause. Some forward-thinking companies are encouraging employees to walk while conducting meetings or to use a stepper or treadmill while having phone meetings. Others are supplying pedometers and encouraging staff to walk at least 10,000 steps a day.

4. Varied. Switch it up to keep the exercise from becoming tedious and to keep all of your muscle groups engaged. Walk one day, ride a bike another, plug in an exercise DVD or lift weights another. Listen to music, books or inspirational information while you move.

5. Purposeful. Walk or bike your errands or park further away from your destinations to get your daily exercise. (One of my clients worked on the thirty-fourth floor of a high-rise. He agreed to get off at the thirtieth floor and walk up four floors daily as a way to add activity.)

6. Distracting. Forget you are exercising by walking while talking with a friend, or power walking on a treadmill while watching TV, a DVD, or talking to someone on the phone. (One of my clients made her daily call to her elderly mother while she walked on the treadmill.)

7. Connected to some kind of (non-food) reward or accountability. Give yourself a monetary reward or a token that relates to a bigger reward connected to achieving your exercise goals. Tie exercise to reading or doing something pleasurable that you may not take time for on a regular basis. Give yourself a big pat on the back when you have completed what you set out to do. It's important to get immediate positive feedback for following through, especially when it's new or something you don't really yet want to do.

Once my clients begin to move, they quickly see the value as they feel better, move with less effort, develop more flexibility, see and feel their bodies change shape, sleep more soundly, and have more energy. Many go on to achieve their weight loss goals and/or improve their health. The same can be true for you.

Chapter 2:

What to Eat to be Trim and Healthy

Many of my students and private weight-management clients appreciate knowing what constitutes a healthy food plan. We are what we eat. Think about it - what we ingest becomes the cell structure of our brains, nervous systems, immune systems, bones, organs, muscles, etc. When we eat healthy food, we become healthier.

The constant controversy in the media about what is healthy and what we should be eating, however, can be confusing at best. Many of my cooking class participants and private clients are unsure of what to eat to be healthy after hearing and reading so many seemingly conflicting theories.

To simplify this issue, almost everyone in the health field agrees that a healthy diet consists of:

- an abundance of vegetables and fruits
- mostly whole grains
- some lean protein
- mostly whole foods or less processed foods, with few artificial ingredients and chemicals
- no or very few added sugars
- good fats, and
- high fiber

There are many different theories about what, how and when to eat, and it may take some trial and error to discover what works best for you. Generally, the following percentages and amounts are recommended as a daily goal:

Carbohydrates

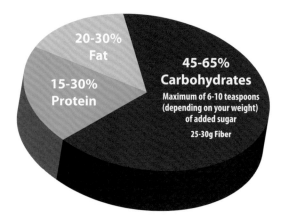

20-30% Fat

15-30% Protein

45-65% Carbohydrates
Maximum of 6-10 teaspoons (depending on your weight) of added sugar
25-30g Fiber

Breads, pastas, cereals, grains, vegetables, legumes, fruit and sugars are considered sources of carbohydrates. They give our cells energy, and like any extra calories we may consume, they are stored as fat if we consume too many of them. Fiber is found in carbohydrates. Your goal should be to eat 25 to 30 grams of fiber throughout the day because it:

- improves blood sugar levels
- helps weight control

- may reduce risk of type 2 diabetes
- may reduce risk of Irritable Bowel Syndrome and diverticular disease
- helps reduce constipation
- lowers cholesterol
- is linked to lower risk of heart disease and
- binds toxins and helps eliminate them, offering protection from cancer

Fiber can be found in beans and peas, whole grains, fruits and vegetables. Find the amount of fiber per serving on the nutrition label or, if the food does not have a label (such as individual fruits and vegetables), check online at www.commonsensehealth. org and scroll to "Foods High in Fiber & Fiber Rich Foods" for the fiber content. Foods considered to be high in fiber have at least 5 grams of fiber per serving. Those that are considered to be a good source have 2.5 to 4 grams of fiber per serving.

Added sugars are simple carbohydrates. Besides "sugar", other names for added sugars include cane sugar, corn sweetener, corn syrup, glucose, high-fructose corn syrup, honey, malt syrup, and sucrose, as well as many others. Scan the list of ingredients of the food or drink to find the added sugar, as ingredients are listed in descending order by weight. Reading the list of ingredients can give you an idea of whether the food contains a lot of sugar, just a bit or none. Each 4 grams of added sugar equals one teaspoon. Most Americans consume more than 22 teaspoons (88 grams or 335 calories) of added sugar per day. My cooking class students are always shocked to learn that most 12 ounce sodas contain 10 or more teaspoons of added sugar. Not only do added sugars supply extra empty calories and help cause tooth decay, they also increase triglyceride levels, possibly contributing to heart disease. Some research suggests that eating too much sugar can play havoc with your immune system. Six to ten teaspoons is the recommended maximum amount, relative to body size.

Fats

You probably know the importance of eliminating trans fats from your diet and lowering saturated fats, but you may wonder which fats are good for you. Most in the health field agree that the best fats are monounsaturated and polyunsaturated fats found in vegetable oils (including olive oil), avocados, nuts, seeds and fish. Increasing the amount of omega-3 fats (a type of polyunsaturated fat) reduces inflammation and may help lower your risk of chronic diseases such as heart disease, stroke, cancer, arthritis and numerous other neurodegenerative diseases. Omega-3 fats are found predominantly in cold-water fish, including salmon and sardines, as well as in plant sources such as flaxseeds, walnuts, whole grains, legumes, nuts and green leafy vegetables. For more on omega-3 fatty acids, see the introduction to the Seafood Entrées in Chapter 11.

Protein

The best protein sources are those that are low in fat and include lean meat, poultry and fish. Other good sources include legumes (beans and peas), soy, eggs, nuts and seeds, milk and milk products, grains and some vegetables.

Many Americans eat too much protein due to large portion sizes, but I have found that many of my women students and clients don't eat enough and often feel hungry throughout the day. How much protein should you consume each day? One of the ways to determine how much you need is to multiply your current weight in pounds by 0.37. This is the minimum number of grams of protein that you should eat on a daily basis. According to this method, a person who weighs 200 pounds will need about 74 grams a day. As a person loses weight, he/she will need less protein.

Another method is to use a percentage (usually 15 - 30%) of calories used throughout the day. Larger and more active people need more calories and protein relatively. A person who weighs 200 pounds and burns 500 extra calories a day will need approximately 2500 to 3000 calories a day (depending on many factors including gender and amount of lean tissue). The range of protein recommended per day for this person (consuming 2500 calories) would be between 93 and 187 grams. Protein is not stored in the body unlike fat (in fat cells) and glucose (in muscle or liver),

so it is important to eat it regularly to keep your blood sugar level and your hunger at bay. I recommend that my clients have some protein at each meal and snack.

Sodium

Most prepared foods contain a lot of sodium, as it helps to flavor food and is often added as a preservative. The 2010 Dietary Guidelines for Americans recommend limiting sodium to less than 2,300 mg per day, or 1,500 mg if you're age 51 or older, are African-American, or have high blood pressure, diabetes or chronic kidney disease.

Fluids

Most weight loss programs recommend that you drink at least 8 glasses of fluid per day to replace the fluid you lose through breathing, sweating and elimination. Besides replacing fluids, drinking them helps you to feel full, especially when you combine them with a higher-fiber diet. Cut back on caffeine, as it can increase cortisol levels, possibly leading to increased belly fat. Decrease sodas, fruit drinks and diet sodas, as some research shows that the sweetness in the diet drinks makes people crave sweet foods, possibly leading to weight gain.

Vegetables and Fruits

Many people don't eat the recommended five to ten daily servings of fruits and vegetables. Doing so will help you eat fewer calories and improve your health. Vegetables and fruits contain essential vitamins, minerals, and fiber that may help protect you from chronic diseases. Compared with people who consume only small amounts of fruits and vegetables, those who eat more generous amounts are likely to have reduced risk of certain cancers, as well as other chronic diseases, including cardiovascular disease. The fiber in vegetables and fruits also provides a feeling of fullness with fewer calories, which can be very helpful when you are trying to consume fewer calories. Trader Joe's and other stores are doing a great job of making it very easy for us to get all those vegetables and fruits in with pre-washed, peeled, sliced, chopped, and frozen options.

A serving size of vegetables is one half cup cooked or raw vegetables and one cup leafy vegetables. For fruit, it is one medium piece of fruit for most items or a half cup for berries. A serving of dried fruit is one quarter cup.

Here is a list of ideas of how to add fresh produce to your meals and snacks:

- Add fresh spinach and/or dark green leafy vegetables to salads.
- Serve a large salad for dinner and top with chicken, fish, shrimp, tofu or beans for protein.
- Add chopped zucchini, bell peppers, onions or frozen spinach to pasta sauces.
- Use fresh TJ's Stir Fry Vegetables as a salad base.
- Add (thawed) frozen or fresh spinach and kale to omelets.
- Use frozen artichoke hearts, chopped zucchini and tomatoes on pizza recipes or add to salads.
- Snack on snap peas, baby carrots, red pepper, or cucumber with a little hummus or tzatziki.
- Have a vegetable soup as a snack or as an addition to lunch or dinner.
- Add fresh vegetables to premade soups.
- If you have a juicer, juice vegetables and fruits for their abundance of nutrients, vitamins and minerals.
- Grill vegetable kabobs when you barbecue.
- Make gazpacho with fresh tomatoes when they are in season.
- Eat cooked sweet potatoes for a snack .
- Use frozen berries in smoothies.
- Use fruit as a snack or dessert instead of baked goods.
- Add fruit to morning cereal.

Below is a list of fruits and veggies from Trader Joe's that are ready-to-eat from the package, as well as a list of produce that needs a little prep before eating. Both are partial lists and are subject to change as items come and go from TJ's shelves. It's a good idea to rinse ready-to-eat vegetables and fruit as an extra safety measure.

Ready-to-Eat Fruits and Vegetables at Trader Joe's:

- beets, cooked
- cut and peeled carrots
- celery
- cucumbers (need slicing)
- edamame
- sugar snap peas
- salad greens including spinach and organic spinach, hearts of romaine, arugula and salad blends
- vegetable tray

Raw Vegetables from Trader Joe's that Need a Little Prep:

- asparagus
- Asparagus Sauté
- Asian Stir Fry
- Broccoli and Cauliflower Duet
- broccoli florets and baby broccoli
- Broccoli Slaw
- bok choy
- Brussels sprouts
- butternut squash
- cauliflower florets
- corn on the cob
- endive
- fresh herbs
- green beans
- green and yellow beans
- green cabbage, shredded
- Healthy Chopped Vegetable Mix
- kale
- mushrooms and sliced mushrooms
- Stir Fry Vegetables (Napa cabbage, bok choy, broccoli and snow peas)
- Southern Green Blend
- Sweet Potato Spears
- Vegetable Trio (asparagus, Brussels spouts and snap peas)
- zucchini and baby zucchini

Frozen Vegetables

Since frozen vegetables are flash-frozen when picked, they can have more nutrients than fresh vegetables that were picked two weeks earlier. So go ahead and breathe a sigh of relief. With your busy life, frozen vegetables are a lifesaver when you don't always get to the market or store every three to four days.

Regarding organic versus non-organic vegetables and fruits, the bottom line is that foods grown organically are better for us. They have no or fewer pesticides, retain greater nutritional value and give us more health benefits than the same foods grown in a conventional manner.

The top 12 foods that are recommended to purchase organically are: apples, bell peppers, celery, cherries, grapes (imported), kale/collards, nectarines, peaches, pears, potatoes, spinach and strawberries. Those that have no or little pesticide residue (and are therefore safer to purchase if conventionally grown) are asparagus, avocados, bananas, broccoli, cabbage, corn, eggplant, kiwis, mangoes, onions, peas, pineapple and sweet potatoes. Check with the Environmental Working Group for an up-to-date list: www.ewg.org.

Below is a list of plain frozen vegetables you can purchase at Trader Joe's, as well as a list of vegetables with added spices or sauces that have 6 grams or less of fat per serving and 340 mg of sodium or less per serving. These are partial lists that are subject to change as products come and go from the shelves or freezer.

Plain Frozen Vegetables:

- artichoke hearts
- asparagus spears, grilled asparagus spears
- broccoli florets
- Brussels sprouts
- Carrots Rustica (yellow and orange carrots)
- corn
- Fire Roasted Corn
- Organic Super Sweet White Corn
- edamame, shelled and unshelled
- Fire Roasted Bell Peppers and Onions
- organic green beans
- haricot verts (tender young green beans)
- Harvest Hodgepodge (broccoli, carrots, baby corn, mushrooms, water chestnuts, sugar snap peas, red peppers and onions)
- chopped spinach and organic chopped spinach
- Organic Foursome Frozen Vegetables (carrots, corn, green beans and peas)
- sliced leeks
- petite peas
- organic peas
- Mélange à Trios (3 color bell pepper medley)
- Soycutash (corn, edamame and red peppers)
- Vegetable Mélange, (peas, carrots, cauliflower and corn)

Vegetables with Added Spices or Sauces:

- Bean So Green: green beans, cauliflower, broccoli, peas, romanesco and garlic butter
  Per serving: 90 calories, 4 g fat, 5 mg cholesterol, 120 mg sodium, 10 g carbohydrate, 4 g fiber, 3 g protein

- Minted Peas: peas in a butter-mint sauce
  Per serving: 110 calories, 3 g fat, 5 mg cholesterol, 170 mg sodium, 14 g carbohydrate, 5 g fiber, 6 g protein

- Cauliflower Romanesque: basilica cauliflower, romanesco, basil, olive oil, garlic, lemon, and seasonings
  Per serving: 70 calories, 4.5 g fat, 0 mg cholesterol, 170 mg sodium, 6 g carbohydrate, 2 g fiber, 2 g protein

- Honey Glazed Roasted Carrots and Parsnips
  Per serving: 140 calories, 6 g fat, 5 mg cholesterol, 340 mg sodium, 22 g carbohydrate, 4 g fiber, 1 g protein

- Country Potatoes with Haricot Verts and Wild Mushrooms
  Per serving: 130 calories, 6 g fat, 0 mg cholesterol, 300 mg sodium, 18 g carbohydrate, 3 g fiber, 2 g protein

- Roasted Potatoes with Roasted Peppers and Onions
  Per serving: 70 calories, 1 g fat, 0 mg cholesterol, 340 mg sodium, 14 g carbohydrate, 3 g fiber, 2 g protein

- Fire Roasted Vegetables with Balsamic Butter Sauce: baby carrots, green beans, bell pepper strips, mushrooms and pearl onions with balsamic butter
  Per serving: 70 calories, 5 g fat, 10 mg cholesterol, 200 mg sodium, 5 g carbohydrate, 1 g fiber, 1 g protein

Tips for Successful Weight Loss

Visualize yourself at your lower weight and shape at least a couple of times daily. Choose regular times during the day to focus on your new self. What will you be wearing, with which activity will you be involved and how will you feel about yourself? Then work toward making that your reality, with the understanding that every time you choose the healthier option you are closer to that goal. You might want to find a picture that depicts the new you and post it in a prominent place to remind yourself of what you want.

Be realistic about your goal and reward yourself for those specific behaviors you've undertaken that will help you reach your goal. We need immediate reinforcement for doing behaviors that are more difficult for us to do. For instance, if you aren't someone who usually exercises, reward yourself immediately after completing exercise with a star or sticker on the calendar, or give yourself a dollar or more in a jar that you can spend on something for yourself after you reach a certain dollar amount. One of my clients bought herself something she really wanted and then "earned" it by giving herself points for practicing specific helpful behaviors - and she lost weight at the same time.

Preplan your meals and snacks. Writing down what you plan to eat for the day can be helpful in many ways: it helps you to be less vulnerable to impulse eating, and it helps you to actually plan and prepare your day's meals and snacks, thus reducing the amount you might eat while searching for something to put together.

Choose to be with people who have healthy eating and exercise habits. It will be easier to follow through on your intentions to eat more healthfully and exercise when you are with others who also eat healthfully and exercise regularly. Maybe you can walk at lunchtime with a co-worker or choose a healthy place to have lunch with a fellow lighter eater. Perhaps you could plan family activities and celebrations that are action-oriented rather than just food-oriented.

When eating at restaurants, eat half your meal (depending on the meal - you may want to eat less than half) and ask yourself if you are still hungry. (It takes at least 20 minutes for the body to register that it has eaten.) If you're satisfied, ask for a take-home container or, if you don't want to take it home, ask that your plate be removed so that you aren't tempted to continue to eat when you aren't hungry. One of my clients pours salt on the part of the meal that is leftover so it will be unappealing. I always say, "Whatever works!"

Chapter 3:

How Trader Joe's Can Help You Lose a Pound a Week

Most clients I work with are surprised to realize how few calories they need to maintain their present weight, especially if they do not exercise or weight-train regularly.

As a starting point, try to figure out how many calories you need to maintain your present weight. The easiest way is to estimate that your body uses about 10 calories per pound of body weight. (To get a more accurate estimate of how many calories you burn, have your body composition tested. Many gyms, fitness centers and YMCAs offer this noninvasive test, which calculates how much lean tissue you have and then how many calories your body burns daily.)

If you suspect that your metabolism is slow, use a factor of 8 or 9 calories per pound of body weight. (Unfortunately, people who have slow metabolisms must eat less to maintain their weight, but regular strength training can improve metabolism.)
For example, a woman who weighs 175 pounds needs approximately 1,750 calories per day plus the calories she spends

exercising to maintain her weight. If she walks 3 miles per day above and beyond her normal activity level, she will need approximately 2050 calories per day to maintain her weight. Below is a chart from the American College of Sports Medicine that shows the approximate number of calories burned for various weights and speeds of walking per hour. You will find the approximate number of calories burned for other activities and body weights at www.nutristrategy.com/caloriesburned.htm.

To Lose One Pound a Week

To lose one pound a week, there must be a deficit of 3,500 calories per week from either your food intake, an increase in activity, or a combination of both. Averaging that deficit over a week's time works out to be 500 calories less per day. The easiest way to do that is to eat 250 to 300 calories less and increase activity by 250 to 300 calories per day.

If you keep records of what you eat for a few days, it might be easy to see where you can cut the extra 250 to 300 calories. Is it the morning latte, the bowl of ice cream while you are watching television at night, the goodies in the office break room, the extra bread and butter at dinner, the wine and cheese when you get home from work or the snacks from the vending machine at work?

To Lose Half-a-Pound a Week

The same idea above is true for losing half-a-pound a week. In this case, you need to reduce calories and/or increase exercise by 250 calories per day.

Weight Loss Example

If a woman weighs 175 pounds and wants to lose a pound a week, she will need to decrease her caloric intake by 250 to 300 calories and increase her activity by 250 to 300 calories per day. If she decreases her caloric intake by 300 calories, eats approximately 1450 calories, and increases her activity by 200 calories, she, in theory, will lose approximately one pound a week.

Calories Burned While Walking (1 hour)

	130 lb	150 lb	180 lb	205 lb
Walking, under 2.0 mph, very slow	118	141	163	186
Walking 2.0 mph, slow	148	176	204	233
Walking 2.5 mph	177	211	245	279
Walking 3.0 mph, moderate	195	232	270	307
Walking 3.5 mph, brisk pace	224	267	311	354
Walking 3.5 mph, uphill	354	422	490	558
Walking 4.0 mph, very brisk	295	352	409	465
Walking 4.5 mph	372	443	515	586
Walking 5.0 mph	472	563	654	745

Menu Planning for 1400 Calories per Day

Planning your menu and shopping from a list will help ease the early evening "What's for dinner?" panic as well as save you time and money from eating at restaurants or getting take-out. When planning your menu, take into account your schedule, evening events, and family plans. Make sure that you have variety in your meals. The more variety, the more nutrients you'll take in. Having more variety may also help you to be more interested in and excited about your menu, helping you to stay with your commitment to make healthier choices.

If you find that you are losing more than one percent of your body weight on a regular basis, increase your calories. If you under-eat regularly, your body may take it as a hint that you are starving and may slow your metabolism, making it harder to lose.

Here are my recommendations for daily meals and snacks totaling approximately 1400 calories:

- Breakfast: 300 calories
- Lunch: 400 calories
- Dinner: 500 calories
- Snacks: Two 100-calorie snacks during the day (see list of 100-calorie snack suggestions on pages 44 to 45)

You can put together any combination of meals that you like from the recipes in this book, or you can follow the suggested weekly menu plans in the back of the book. Check the appendix on pages 195 to 207 for two examples of a week's worth of menus and corresponding grocery lists for the approximately 1400 calories per day meal plans. Usually, two sources of calcium are included in each day's menu. Suggestions on increasing the number of calories to 1600 and 1800 follow the weekly plans. The menus consist of some recipes and some ready-to-eat products, which you may want to use on days when you have less time.

Regarding the recipes in this book, breakfast recipes vary from serving 1 to 4 people, lunch from 2 to 4, and dinner is almost always (with a few exceptions) intended to serve 4. So, depending on the number of servings you are preparing, you might want to make less, have leftovers for lunch or dinner the next day, or if freezable, freeze the meal for another day.

About the Recipes in This Book

The recipes presented in this book were created to help you, a Trader Joe's shopper, choose foods that will enable you to make positive changes in how you nourish yourself, or perhaps continue feeding yourself well while losing weight. The products and recipes chosen feature the recommended foods suggested in this chapter. The recipes are low in added sugar, fat, cholesterol, sodium, calories, preservatives, artificial flavors and colorings; they are a good source of fiber and nutrients, and if appropriate to the meal course, they have a good amount of protein. When possible, a bread or grain product with a higher source of fiber was chosen for the recipe ingredient or accompaniment. Suggested meal accompaniments are made for main entrée recipes, and I've designated the recipes as "quick" (takes a few minutes) or "super-quick" (takes almost no time) to help you plan according to your schedule. The suggested weekly menus and shopping lists presented in the appendix will help you further simplify the process of planning and preparing your healthy meals and snacks (more available online at www. HealthyTraderJoes.com).

Trader Joe's advertises that their private label items contain no artificial flavors, colors or preservatives, no genetically modified ingredients, no MSG and no added trans fats. Their policy is that if you don't like a product you can bring it back for a refund. They provide shopping guides online for products that are vegan, vegetarian, fat-free, "quick meal", Kosher, low-sodium and gluten-free.

Basic information regarding the calculation of nutrition analysis in each recipe

- First ingredients were used wherever a choice is given (such as 1/2 cup plain nonfat yogurt or sour cream).

- TJ's chicken broth (Organic Free Range and Free Range) each have 570 mg of sodium per cup. TJ's Low Sodium Chicken Broth has 70 mg of sodium per

cup. The first two are used in the recipes unless the Low Sodium version is listed in the recipe.

- Most of the products used in the recipes are available at Trader Joe's. Some common ingredients are listed generically and some are listed as Trader Joe's products, so that you will know they are available at Trader Joe's.

- Nutritional analysis does not include optional ingredient items or "Options" suggestions following recipes.

- Recipe analysis was calculated using information from Trader Joe's packages, as well as several FDA sources. While they are very good estimates per serving, they may not be exact, depending on many factors.

- Weighted amounts do not necessarily equal volume amounts and vice versa. For example, 12 weighted ounces of broccoli does not equal 1 ½ cups of broccoli and vice versa.

Other recipe information:

- I have included information on lowering sodium in many of the recipes as a benefit to those of you who are on lower-sodium diets or have been told to cut back on the amount of sodium you consume.

- Always choose organic soy products, if available, as they are guaranteed to not be genetically manipulated and to be free of herbicides.

• Dairy-free, gluten-free, vegan and vegetarian recipes are noted as such:

 Dairy-free

 Gluten-free

 Vegan

 Vegetarian

Every effort was made to insure that the designations are accurate with the specific products used; however, products and ingredients change, so it would be in your best interest to check product ingredients if you have something specific you, or those you are preparing meals for, are avoiding. Trader Joe's supplies a list of No Gluten, Vegan and Vegetarian foods online at www.TraderJoes.com. Some stores have copies of each available for shoppers.

You will notice that some recipes have suggestions on how to easily modify a recipe in order for it to be gluten-free, dairy-free, vegetarian or vegan. There are also some suggestions to alter vegetarian meals, making them non-vegetarian.

• The products change often at Trader Joe's. Every effort was made to ensure that at the time of printing the products included in the recipes were currently available at Trader Joe's. If you find that one of the ingredients is no longer available, I hope that you will use a suggestion on the options list or substitute something similar.

• **Weight Watcher Points**™ for recipes included in this book are available online at my website: www.HealthyTraderJoes.com.

Tips for Successful Weight Loss

The more that you practice good eating and exercise behaviors, the easier it will be to choose those behaviors over and over again until they become habit. It's a self-reinforcing cycle, and it works the same way for behaviors that are not helpful to you.

What you perceived as "good" may change. I am always pleasantly surprised when my clients exclaim after about three weeks of working together how much better they feel due to eating lighter fare and engaging in some exercise. They are motivated to continue eating well because they feel so much better. The restaurant with unlimited servings becomes less enticing as they focus on how they want to feel after a meal by eating less. The second helping of extra rich dessert at that party loses its appeal as they focus on how they want to look and feel in their smaller size clothes the next day.

Be aware of your triggers to overeat. What compels you to eat when you aren't even hungry? Is it a certain feeling, thought, situation or person? You might want to make a list of pleasurable activities that take just a few minutes to do in place of eating when you aren't hungry but want to eat. For example, listen to music, read, write a note, call a friend, write down six reasons why you want to lose weight, search for something you want to know about on the internet, take a short walk, take six deep breaths, read the comics, water the plants, pet your animal(s), write down five things you are grateful for, or even pop bubble wrap (one of my favorites.)

Ask those you live and work with to help you by keeping foods that you find tempting out of your sight or even to hide them where you won't find them. For example, if a member of your household has goodies every night while they are watching TV, you could ask them to put the packaging away and not leave the goodies on the counter where you might see them. Or you might request that some foods you find difficult to resist not be brought into the house. For a time, I could not resist dipping a spoon into peanut butter a few times a day and ingesting hundreds of extra calories. Until I learned to eat reasonable amounts of it, we didn't have it in the house.

Recognize your resistances to change when you find that you aren't making the changes necessary to lose despite desperately wanting to fit into your smaller size clothes. We usually have good reasons to be in resistance, although we may be unaware of those reasons. Once discovered, the resistances can be acknowledged and dealt with. For example, one client was unaware that he felt he would be betraying his overweight father if he were to become lighter. Another discovered that she thought her friends would feel abandoned if she ate more nutritiously than they did. And still another thought she would be seen as shallow and pretentious if she became slimmer and spruced up her appearance.

Chapter 4:
Breakfast

You've heard that breakfast is the most important meal of the day. Many people skip it because they don't have enough time to prepare and eat it. Or they think they can save calories by waiting until lunch. If you are one of those who skip breakfast, you may not realize that having protein and fiber in the morning help control your blood sugar throughout the day. That means you can avoid the "hungries", which could help curb impulsive food choices that can interfere with your weight loss success.

Do your best to make it convenient to have breakfast daily. Some of the following suggestions may help:

- Take some of these breakfast ingredients to work, and eat them at your desk or during a morning break.
- Rotate between two or three choices during the week. Doing so lessens the options, making the choices easier as well as simplifying your weekly grocery list.
- Make breakfast the night before and have it ready to eat or drink.
- Keep hard boiled eggs in the fridge, and grab them on your way out.
- If preparing breakfast is not an option, map out where you can get

something good for you and pick it up on your way, or use some of the quick option ideas below.

Instant and very quick options:

In a pinch, meal replacement bars are better than eating nothing or a pastry high in sugar and fat. The bar should have at least 2 grams of fiber and at least 8 grams of protein. It should also be free of refined sugars, refined grains, trans fats and artificial sweeteners.

Here are some bars and meals from Trader Joe's that meet the guidelines above:

- Larabar (search for the ones with higher protein)
- Luna Bar (your Trader Joe's may also carry Luna Protein Bars)
- Kind bars
- Clif Builder's Bars
- TJ's Oatmeal Complete instant oatmeal
- Whole grain bread, toasted with ricotta cheese or cottage cheese and applesauce, or with Ricotta-Peanut Butter Spread (see recipe on page 32).

Yonola

Here's an easy combination of yogurt and granola to get your day started.

Serves 1

1 cup TJ's Plain Nonfat Yogurt
½ cup berries, fresh or frozen
½ cup TJ's Low Fat Granola

Combine the ingredients together in a small serving bowl and gently blend with a spoon.

Per serving: *282 calories, 1.6 g fat, 0 mg cholesterol, 200 mg sodium, 54 g carbohydrate, 10 g fiber, 13 g protein*

Options:
Use high-fiber cereal, such as Kashi GoLean Crunch! or Uncle Sam's Cereal in place of granola.

 Vegetarian

Yoats

This is an easy, filling breakfast to take with you when you're on the run or to eat later in the morning when you have more time. The uncooked oatmeal absorbs moisture from the yogurt and gives it a chewy texture. It's a very nutritious way to begin your day.

Serves 1

¾ cup TJ's Nonfat Plain Yogurt
⅓ cup regular (not instant) oatmeal
½ cup frozen blueberries, optional
Stevia to taste, optional

Add the oatmeal to the yogurt and stir until combined. Let the mixture sit for at least 5 minutes. Add blueberries or other fruit, if desired.

Per serving: *255 calories, 2.3 g fat, 0 mg cholesterol, 128 mg sodium, 44.3 g carbohydrate, 6 g fiber, 12.2 g protein*

Options:
- Substitute other chopped fruit or berries in place of blueberries.
- Add chopped walnuts or almonds.
- Add a tablespoon of ground flaxseeds.

 *Gluten-free if oatmeal is certified gluten-free

Vegetarian

Vegetable Omelet with Toast

Here's a great way to start your day with lots of vegetables and protein. Use chopped zucchini, mushrooms, onions, or 2 cups chopped kale, spinach or TJ's Southern Greens Blend.

Serves 1

TJ's Extra Virgin Olive Oil Spray
3 egg whites or ½ cup egg
    whites from carton
1 cup fresh or frozen vegetables
2 tablespoons shredded low-fat
    Cheddar cheese

1. Spray a nonstick skillet with cooking spray and place over medium heat.
2. Add the vegetables and cook for about 3 minutes, stirring occasionally, until the vegetables can be easily pierced with a fork.
3. Add the egg whites and stir until eggs are cooked, about 2 minutes.
4. Add the cheese and stir. Serve with one slice whole wheat toast (included in nutritional analysis).

Per serving: 260 calories, 7 g fat, 15 mg cholesterol, 385 mg sodium, 29 g carbohydrate, 8 g fiber, 26 g protein

Options:

- For an Italian flavor, use 1 tablespoon fresh grated Parmesan in place of the cheese, and add 1 tablespoon chopped fresh basil or 1 teaspoon dried basil. Add 2 tablespoons marinara.
- Omit the cheese for a dairy-free and lower fat version.

 Vegetarian

Veggie Frittata Muffins

Make these ahead of time and refrigerate or freeze for grab-and-go breakfasts for the whole family. They have a good amount of protein and get you started on your vegetable servings for the day. To increase fiber, add a couple of tablespoons of ground flaxseed to the eggs, or have with a piece of whole wheat toast for an extra 3 to 5 grams of fiber.

Serves 6

1 (16 ounce) container egg whites or 8 egg whites
1 whole egg
⅓ cup skim milk
½ to 1 teaspoon TJ's 21 Seasoning Salute
½ cup loosely packed fresh spinach leaves, chopped
½ cup broccoli, diced
½ zucchini, diced
4 mushrooms, diced
6 leaves fresh basil or 1 frozen Dorot Basil cube
2 tablespoons freshly grated Parmigiano-Reggiano cheese or Parmesan cheese
TJ's Extra Virgin Olive Oil Spray
1 slice of TJ's 100% Whole Grain Fiber Wheat Bread, or whole wheat bread

1. Preheat oven to 350ºF.
2. In a large nonstick skillet, over medium-high heat, spray olive oil spray and add the spinach, broccoli, zucchini and mushrooms. Cook for 5 minutes, until softened. Allow to cool slightly.
3. In a medium bowl, whisk eggs, milk, and seasoning. Stir in the cooked vegetables; add 1 tablespoon of the grated cheese and stir to combine.
4. Spray a muffin tin with cooking spray. Fill each cup about 1/2 full. Makes 6 oversize muffins or 9-10 regular-size muffins.
5. Tear the slice of whole wheat bread into the same number of pieces as muffins and drop on top of the muffins. Sprinkle with the remaining grated cheese and bake for 35-40 minutes, until the egg is no longer soft or wet.

Per serving: 168 calories, 1.8 g fat, 35 mg cholesterol, 176 mg sodium, 4.7 g carbohydrate, 1.3 g fiber, 11.5 g protein

Options:
- Add ½ cup onion when cooking vegetables.
- Add 2 tablespoons ground flaxseeds.

 Vegetarian

Ricotta-Peanut Butter Breakfast Spread

Trader Joe's now carries fat-free ricotta cheese, a good source of protein and calcium. Take this to work for a desk-top breakfast or spread it on bread or crackers as a snack. It will keep for a few days in the fridge. It also makes a good sandwich filling for lunch boxes. Adapted from *Vegetarian Times* cookbook.

**Serves 4,
about ¼ cup per serving**

1 cup TJ's Fat Free Ricotta Cheese
2 tablespoons TJ's Peanut Butter or
    Almond Butter, no salt added
½ tablespoon honey
⅛ teaspoon almond extract
¼ teaspoon vanilla extract
⅛ teaspoon cinnamon

Add all of the ingredients together and blend. Spread onto whole grain toast, toaster waffles or baby bagels. Or serve as a fruit dip.

Per serving: *100 calories, 4 g fat, 0 mg cholesterol, 76 mg sodium, 5.25 g carbohydrate, 1.75 g fiber, 7.75 g protein*

 Gluten-free

 Vegetarian

Salmon-Caper Breakfast Pockets

Salmon for breakfast? Why not? This breakfast gives you lots of protein to get you going and will last you until lunchtime. Plus, it's easy! Prepare the cheese spread the night before and assemble the sandwich the next morning.

Serves 4

⅓ cup TJ's Whipped Light Cream
   Cheese or TJ's Light
   Cream Cheese
3 tablespoon capers, drained
1 ½ teaspoons lemon zest
2 TJ's Whole Wheat Pita Pockets,
   halved
7 ounces cooked salmon (fresh or
   canned), flaked
2 Roma tomatoes, chopped
2 cups arugula leaves

1. Blend cream cheese, capers and
   lemon together in a small bowl.
2. For each pita half, spread ¼ of
   cream cheese mix on one side.
   Arrange a quarter of the salmon
   on top; add ¼ tomato and tuck
   in ½ cup arugula.

Per serving (using canned salmon): 180 calories, 6.3 g fat, 22 mg cholesterol, 330 mg sodium, 16.5 g carbohydrate, 2.8 g fiber, 16 g protein

Options:
- To lower sodium, omit capers.
- Toast pita pockets for a crunchy version.

Veggie Burger Breakfast Sandwich

Compared to a McDonald's Egg McMuffin, this tasty breakfast sandwich saves you 70 calories, 6 g of fat, 235 mg cholesterol, and 260 mg sodium, and it delivers 5 more grams of fiber! It takes just minutes to prepare.

Serves 1

TJ's Extra Virgin Italian Olive Oil Spray
1 Dr. Praeger's California Veggie Burger
2 egg whites or ⅓ cup egg whites from carton
1 slice large tomato
1 TJ's English Muffin, British Whole Wheat

1. In a nonstick pan over medium heat, spray vegetable spray and add veggie burger. Crumble the patty gently with a fork. Add egg whites and stir until eggs are cooked, about 2 minutes.
2. Toast the English muffin.
3. Place egg scramble on the bottom of the English muffin and top with the tomato and other half of the muffin.

Per serving: 234 calories, 6.7 g fat, 0 mg cholesterol, 590 mg sodium, 30 g carbohydrate, 7 g fiber, 18 g protein

Options:

- Use 1 ounce low-fat sausage patty in place of burger.
- Omit veggie burger and add 1 ounce smoked salmon.

 Vegetarian

Super-Charged Oatmeal

Trader Joe's protein powders are made from either whey, soy or hemp. If none of those work for you, purchase other types of protein powder, including rice protein, at a vitamin or health food store.

Serves 1

1 cup water
½ cup rolled oats (not instant)
1 scoop TJ's Soy Protein Powder
Dash of cinnamon

Prepare oatmeal according to package directions. Add protein powder and stir until combined.

Per serving: *210 calories, 3.2 g fat, 0 mg cholesterol, 140 mg sodium, 25 g carbohydrate, 4 g fiber, 19.5 g protein*

Options:

- Use ½ cup cottage cheese in place of the protein powder.
- Add ¼ to ½ cup fresh or frozen berries.
- Use other grains besides oatmeal such as brown rice, quinoa and/or millet.
- Add 1 tablespoon ground flaxseeds.

 *Gluten-free if you use Bob's Red Mill Oatmeal or other oatmeal certified gluten-free

 *Vegan if use vegan protein powder

Fruit Smoothie for Two

A good way to get a quick breakfast before school or work so your brain can function optimally throughout the morning.

Serves 2

2 large frozen bananas
1 cup frozen blueberries
1 cup unsweetened almond milk
2 tablespoons TJ's Raw Almond
   Butter
1 cup ice cubes

Combine ingredients in a blender or food processor. Blend all ingredients on high until thick and creamy. Add more nut milk if needed.

Per serving: *270 calories, 10 g fat, 0 mg cholesterol, 71 mg sodium, 50 g carbohydrate, 7.65 g fiber, 6.6 g protein*

Options:
- Add a scoop of protein powder for a higher-protein breakfast.
- Use peaches, strawberries, blackberries, mangos or pineapple in place of blueberries.
- Add 2 tablespoons ground flaxseeds.
- Make this with cashew butter or tahini instead of almond butter.
- Omit almond butter to reduce fat.
- For a non-vegan option and to increase protein, use nonfat milk.

 Gluten-free

 Vegan

Breakfast Burrito

A little spice to start your day! This also makes a great high-protein afternoon snack.

Serves 1

TJ's Extra Virgin Italian Olive Oil
   Spray
1 egg and 2 whites, or ½ cup egg
   whites from a carton
¼ cup salsa
½ cup chopped zucchini
1 slice low-fat mozzarella or
   Cheddar cheese
1 corn tortilla
A few drops of hot sauce, optional
1 tablespoon chopped fresh
   cilantro, optional

1. In a nonstick skillet, sprayed
   with cooking spray over
   medium-high heat, scramble
   egg whites with salsa and
   zucchini.
2. Add cheese and cook until
   cheese is melted.
3. Meanwhile, heat tortilla in the
   microwave, oven or toaster
   oven. When eggs are cooked
   serve them in the warm tortilla.

Per serving: 257 calories, 10 g fat, 215 mg cholesterol, 560 mg sodium, 22 g carbohydrate, 3.5 g fiber, 24.6 g protein

Options:
- Add ¼ cup black or cannellini beans to add fiber and protein
- To give this an Italian flavor, use marinara sauce in place of salsa, use part skim mozzarella as the cheese, and serve in a whole wheat tortilla with a few leaves of chopped basil.

 Gluten-free

 Vegetarian

On-the-Go Protein Shake

Make this drink the night before and put it in the fridge so you can grab it, shake it and drink it on your way.

Serves 1

2 scoops TJ's Whey Vanilla Protein
  Powder
1 cup nonfat milk
½ cup frozen berries
Dash of cinnamon, optional

Add all of the ingredients together in a jar or container with a tight-fitting lid and shake until blended.

Per serving: *203 calories, 3 g fat, 45 mg cholesterol, 106 mg sodium, 39 g carbohydrate, 5.8 g fiber, 21 g protein*

Options:
- Use other protein powders in place of whey protein powder.
- Use nut milk in place of nonfat milk.
- Use chocolate protein powder in place of vanilla and add ½ banana and 1 tablespoon peanut butter.
- Add a tablespoon of ground flaxseeds.

 Gluten-free

 Vegetarian

High Protein, High Fiber Cereal

Many high fiber cereals are also high in sugar. When you are looking at food labels, note that each 4 g of sugar equals 1 teaspoon of sugar. Uncle Sam cereal has 10 g of fiber and only 1 gram of sugar.

Serves 1

¾ cup Uncle Sam cereal or other
   high-fiber cereal
1 cup nonfat milk
1 scoop plain or vanilla protein
   powder

After pouring the cereal into a bowl, combine the milk and protein powder in a glass or jar and stir or shake to blend. Pour over the cereal.

Per serving: *330 calories, 6 g fat, 18 mg cholesterol, 168 mg sodium, 55 g carbohydrate, 10 g fiber, 23 g protein*

Options:
- Use rice, hemp, soy or almond milk in place of nonfat milk.
- Add fruit.
- Add vanilla or almond extract for extra flavor.

 Vegetarian

Tofu Scramble

My tasters thought these were scrambled eggs and I didn't tell them differently until they had eaten them. My son, Ross, suggested serving them in a pita pocket with hot sauce.

Serves 4

TJ's Extra Virgin Olive Oil Spray
1 medium onion, diced or 1 cup
    TJ's Diced Onions
1 carrot, diced, or ¾ cup
    TJ's Shredded Carrots
1 stalk celery, diced
1 (14 ounce) package TJ's Organic
    Firm Tofu, drained and
    crumbled
1 teaspoon turmeric
1 teaspoon cumin
Salt and freshly-ground pepper
    to taste
Dash of TJ's 21 Seasoning Salute,
    optional
¼ cup chopped fresh parsley or
    cilantro
1 tablespoon balsamic vinegar
½ tablespoon TJ's Reduced
    Sodium Soy Sauce or tamari
2 TJ's Whole Wheat Pita Pockets,
    sliced in half
1 medium tomato, chopped
Hot sauce, optional

1. In a large skillet sprayed with olive oil cooking spray, sauté onions for about 3 minutes, until translucent. Add carrots and celery; sauté 3 more minutes.
2. Add tofu, crumbling with your hands or a fork, spices, cilantro, vinegar and soy sauce and continue to stir 3 to 4 more minutes.
3. Place tofu scramble evenly into 4 pita pockets. Add tomato and hot sauce, if desired.

Per serving: 117 calories, 6.1g fat, 0 mg cholesterol, 145 mg sodium, 16.3 carbohydrate, 3.8 g fiber, 12.5 protein

Options:
- Add fresh spinach, kale or other vegetables such as red bell pepper, potatoes, or green onions, mushrooms, etc.
- Add hot sauce to the tofu mixture before placing in the pita pockets.

 *Gluten-free if you use tamari in place of soy sauce and wrap tofu mixture in TJ's Brown Rice Tortillas in place of pita pockets.

Vegan

Overnight Steel Cut Oats

It usually takes about 30 to 40 minutes to cook steel cut oats on the stove and about 15 minutes in the microwave. Try this slow-cooker version that allows you to put it together the night before and cook overnight. If you're only serving one, store the other servings in the fridge and reheat in the microwave.

Serves 4

4 cups water
1 cup steel cut oats, such as McCann's Irish Brand or Country Choice Irish Style Steel Cut Oats

1. Place the water and oats in a glass, oven-proof bowl that holds 5 to 6 cups and fits into your slow-cooker so that the lid fits.
2. Fill the slow cooker with water to a little more than halfway. Set the bowl of oats and water in the slow cooker and add water, if necessary, so that the water reaches about the same height on the outside of the bowl as the cooking water inside the bowl.
3. Place the lid on the slow cooker and cook on LOW for 8 to 9 hours.

Per serving: 150 calories, 2.5 g fat, 0 mg cholesterol, 0 mg sodium, 27 g carbohydrate, 3 fiber, 4 g protein

Options:
- Substitute 2 cups of milk for 2 cups of water.
- Add ½ cup dried fruit and cinnamon.

🚫 *Gluten-free if you use certified gluten-free oats

🌱 Vegan

Chapter 5

Healthy Grab-and-Go Lunches and 100-Calorie Snack Ideas

These prepared Trader Joe's products make lunch preparation super easy. (These products could also be used for a quick dinner for one.) Just grab and go, or purchase these items a few days ahead and keep them refrigerated or frozen. One of the keys to being successful with eating healthy meals and snacks is to have them ready and available when you want to eat in order to avoid impulse eating.

My criteria for choosing these lunch products is that the item be a reasonable serving size, under 400 calories, contain 10 grams of fat or less, and have less than 800 milligrams of sodium per serving. Many of the salads at Trader Joe's could work if you use the dressing sparingly or substitute them with a lower calorie dressing. Check the labels.

While you could put many Trader Joe's products together for lunch or dinner, I've listed only convenience products that are ready to eat.

All of the following meals serve one.

Refrigerated Meals

Chicken Salad - Reduced Fat Chinese Chicken Salad with dressing
340 calories, 4 g fat, 65 mg cholesterol, 710 mg sodium, 42 g carbohydrate, 4 g fiber, 32 g protein

Grilled Chicken Pasta Salad with Mango with dressing
380 calories, 2.5 g fat, 30 g cholesterol, 350 mg sodium, 70 g carbohydrate, 5 g fiber, 22 g protein

Mango, Red Quinoa and Chicken Salad with dressing
240 calories, 10 g fat, 40 mg cholesterol, 610 mg sodium, 20 g carbohydrate, 5 g fiber, 19 g protein

Reduced Fat Southwest Salad with dressing
170 calories, 7 g fat, 10 mg cholesterol, 720 mg sodium, 22 g carbohydrate, 4 g fiber, 8 g protein

Vietnamese Style Chicken Wrap
400 calories, 7 g fat, 25 mg cholesterol, 520 mg sodium, 55 g carbohydrate, 4 g fiber, 21 g protein

Heat-and-Eat Frozen Meals

Garden Vegetable Lasagna
290 calories, 9 g fat, 20 mg cholesterol, 720 mg sodium, 44 g carbohydrate, 13 g protein

Reduced Guilt Baked Ziti
320 calories, 7 g fat, 10 mg cholesterol, 590 mg sodium, 55 g carbohydrate, 3 g fiber, 12 g protein

Reduced Guilt Fillet of Sole
190 calories, 2 g fat, 40 mg cholesterol, 670 mg sodium, 30 g carbohydrate, 3 g fiber, 15 g protein

Reduced Guilt Pizza Primavera
250 calories, 7 g fat, 5 mg cholesterol, 640 mg sodium, 38 g carbohydrate, 2 g fiber, 10 g protein

Reduced Guilt Roasted Vegetable Couscous
250 calories, 5 g fat, 10 mg cholesterol, 670 mg sodium, 30 g carbohydrate, 3 g fiber, 15 g protein

Reduced Guilt Mac and Cheese
270 calories, 6 g fat, 20 mg cholesterol, 540 mg sodium, 4 g carbohydrate, 1 g fiber, 15 g protein

TJ's Chicken Vindaloo
290 calories, 3.5 g fat, 30 mg cholesterol, 590 mg sodium, 47 g carbohydrate, 3 g fiber, 16 g protein

Black Bean and Corn Enchilada (analysis is for whole package - 2 servings)
260 calories, 8 g fat, 0 mg cholesterol, 460 mg sodium, 40 g carbohydrate, 4 g fiber, 8 g protein

Thai Style Massaman Chicken
390 calories, 10 g fat, 30 mg cholesterol, 480 mg sodium, 56 g carbohydrate, 3 g fiber, 17 g protein

Healthy Snacks

Snacks can play a role in keeping you nourished within a daily caloric range. You know your schedule, exertion and hunger levels, so make sure that you are eating healthy food throughout the day, saving room for a reasonable dinner. If you're ravenous when you get home from work, you're likely to overeat. But if you have a pre-planned substantial snack in the afternoon, you're less likely to be starving when you arrive home.

Make sure that your snacks contain some protein to stabilize your blood sugar levels so that you don't get overly hungry between meals. Avoid sugary snacks, as they may cause your blood sugar to go up and then drop, leaving you hungrier. For some people, even eating a piece of fruit without some accompanying protein will cause their blood sugar to rise and fall, leaving them hungry soon after.

The snacks I've chosen are approximately 100 calories each. If your intention is to eat only about 100 calories, be sure to eat only the amount listed, and keep a record of the food you eat. Doing so is one of the most important things you can do to lose weight as well as to maintain weight loss. I often liken it to keeping a monetary budget when people overspend and don't know where the money goes. I have designated those that are gluten-free for those who are avoiding gluten.

100-Calorie Snacks

2 TJ's Turkey Meatballs (100 calories) dipped in marinara sauce (10 calories), mustard, salsa, or any low-fat, low-calorie sauce

2 ounces tuna in water* mixed with 1 tablespoon light mayonnaise and sprinkled with a dash of onion powder, dill, mustard or TJ's 21 Seasoning Salute

1 Light Mini Babybel cheese (50 calories) with 2 ½ Ak Mak whole wheat crackers (57 calories)

½ mini bagel (37 calories) with 2 ounces smoked salmon (66 calories)

1 large graham cracker rectangle (60 calories) with 2 teaspoons peanut butter (66 calories)

¼ package TJ's Savory or Teriyaki Baked Tofu (75 and 80 calories, respectively) and ½ cup snap peas (15 to 20 calories)

1 ½ ounces TJ's Natural Turkey Jerky (90 calories)

½ slice whole wheat bread (40 calories) with ¼ cup fat free ricotta cheese (45 calories) and cinnamon, or 2 tablespoons Ricotta-Peanut Butter Breakfast Spread (50 calories), page 32

Gluten-free 100-Calorie Snacks

½ package (105 calories) TJ's Just a Handful almonds or cashews

1 part skim string cheese stick (80 calories)

2 Light Mini Babybel Cheeses (100 calories)

1 carton TJ's Egg White Salad (100 calories)

½ cup nonfat Greek style yogurt (60 calories) with 8 medium strawberries (45 calories)

A large stalk of celery (10 calories) stuffed with 1 tablespoon peanut butter (100 calories) or 2 tablespoons of soft light cream cheese (70)

1 cup TJ's Latin Style Black Bean Soup (70 calories) with 4 baked tortilla chips (34 calories) or 2 tablespoons of plain nonfat Greek style yogurt (14 calories) on top

½ large red bell pepper (35 calories) or other vegetables dipped in 4 tablespoons TJ's Eggplant Hummus (70 calories)

1 package Roasted Seaweed Snack (60 calories) and ½ carton Egg White Salad (50 calories)

Polenta round slice (1/5) (70 calories) and ¼ cup frozen TJ's Turkey Bolognese (40 calories), heated

1 rice cake (30 calories each) with 2 teaspoons almond butter (66 calories)

1 large hard boiled egg (70 calories)

1 warmed corn tortilla (50-60 calories) and 4 tablespoons TJ's Fat Free Spicy Black Bean Dip (60 calories)

1/3 cup low-fat cottage cheese (53 calories) with cinnamon, and 1/3 cup low-fat fruit yogurt (50 calories)

1/3 cup low-fat cottage cheese (53 calories) with 8 medium strawberries (45 calories)

1 glass 1% fat milk (110 calories)

1 bag TJ's 94% Fat Free Microwave Popcorn
Per bag (6 bags per box): 130 calories, 2 g fat, 0 mg cholesterol, 100 mg sodium, 24 g carbohydrate, 4 g fiber, 3 g protein

1 rice cake (30 calories) with 1 tablespoon low-fat cream cheese (35 calories), and 1 teaspoon each TJ's Corn & Chile Tomato-less Salsa (8 calories) and low sugar apricot preserves (10 calories)

½ cup TJ's O's cereal (55 calories) and ½ cup skim milk (43 calories)

*Make sure you are purchasing canned tuna without soy sauce in the list of ingredients if you want it to be gluten-free.

Chapter 6:
Sandwiches, Wraps, and Fillings

The following recipes make great choices for lunches and light dinners. Many are easy to take with you to the office or wherever you might be at lunchtime. For those of you who want or need to lower the sodium in your diet, I have made sure that the recipes have below 800 mg of sodium per serving and have given ideas in the "options" sections as to how to lower it further, if possible. Your choice of bread can make a difference in the total number of grams of sodium per recipe, as some breads can have a substantial amount of sodium. I recommend wrapping the fillings in lettuce or tortillas, or using lower sodium breads in some of the recipes to decrease sodium. The recipes are arranged in the order of chicken, seafood and vegetarian.

Chicken Sandwich with Secret Sauce

Tired of the same old chicken sandwich? Try my Secret Sauce, a combination of two popular Trader Joe's condiments, to add restaurant-style flavor. Serve with a green salad.

Serves 2

¼ cup TJ's Corn and Chile
   Tomato-Less Salsa
2 tablespoons TJ's Low Fat
   Parmesan Ranch dressing
2 TJ's Whole Wheat Hamburger
   Buns
1 ½ cups (6 ounces) frozen TJ's Just
   Grilled Chicken Strips, thawed;
   or 6 ounces cooked chicken
2 leaves lettuce
2 tomato slices, optional
Ground pepper

1. Mix corn salsa with ranch dressing in a small bowl or measuring cup. Spread it on the bottom half of the bun.
2. Place half of the chicken strips on top of the sauce. Add lettuce and tomato, if using, and sprinkle with pepper. Top with the other half of the bun and serve.

Per serving: 320 calories, 4.25 g fat, 45 mg cholesterol, 740 mg sodium, 30 g carbohydrate, 2.5 g fiber, 23 g protein

Option:
- Substitute a whole wheat tortilla to make into a wrap and to lower sodium.
- Substitute lettuce as a wrap to decrease calories, sodium and carbohydrates.
- Place chicken and dressing on top of salad, instead of a bun.

Mango Chicken Lettuce Wraps

I got a very enthusiastic thumbs up from those who tasted these wraps. They are crunchy and sweet, low in sodium and carbohydrates, and have a good amount of protein to fill you up for the afternoon. This recipe is adapted from one in *Good Housekeeping* magazine.

Serves 4, makes 10 to12 wraps

½ package (8 ounces) frozen TJ's Mango Chunks, or bottled or fresh mango

1 cup peeled and finely chopped jicama

½ cup packed fresh mint leaves, finely chopped

2 tablespoons fresh lime juice

1 tablespoon extra virgin olive oil

1 tablespoon TJ's Sweet Chili sauce or ½ teaspoon Asian Chili Sauce

¼ teaspoon salt, optional

2 cups frozen TJ's Just Grilled Chicken Strips, cut in bite-size pieces; or 2 cups cooked chicken, cut into bite-size pieces

10 to12 Boston lettuce leaves

1. Combine mango, jicama, mint, lime juice, olive oil, chili sauce and salt in a bowl and toss. Add chicken and stir to coat.
2. Place ¼ of the filling onto the middle of each lettuce leaf and wrap each side of the lettuce around the mixture.

Per serving *(If made 10 wraps, serving size is 2 ½ wraps): 162 calories, 4.4 g fat, 2.5 mg cholesterol, 242 mg sodium, 18.6 carbohydrates, 2.5 g fiber, 16.5 g protein*

Options:
- Substitute celery or water chestnuts for jicama.
- Add 4 finely chopped green onions.
- Add ½ to 1 teaspoon cumin.
- Substitute TJ's Papaya Mango Salsa for the jicama, mint, lime juice, olive oil, chili sauce and salt.
- Use corn or whole wheat flour tortillas in place of lettuce.

 Dairy-Free

Chicken Curry with Warm Pita Pockets

Every one of my cooking class participants has loved the taste of this curry sauce. Freeze the leftover curry sauce in a freezable container or bag for next time, as there are no preservatives in any Trader Joe's private label products.

Serves 4

12 ounces TJ's Just Chicken, cut into bite-size pieces; or 12 ounces cooked chicken, cut into bite-sized pieces

½ cup TJ's Yellow Thai Curry Sauce

½ cup snow peas

2 TJ's Whole Wheat Pita Pockets, halved

½ red bell pepper, sliced in slivers, optional

4 fresh basil leaves, chopped

½ cup fresh spinach

2 green onions, diced, optional

1. Preheat oven to 350ºF.
2. Combine the chicken and curry sauce in a saucepan and heat over medium heat for 7 to 8 minutes, adding the snow peas and red pepper, if using, the last 2 minutes. Or combine the chicken and curry sauce in a microwaveable bowl and heat for 2 minutes, adding the snow peas and red pepper, if using, and heating for 1 minute more.
3. While chicken and sauce are heating, heat pita pockets in the oven on a baking sheet.
4. When the filling and bread are warm, place ¼ of the chicken filling in each of the 4 pita pocket halves. Add the basil leaves, spinach and scallions, if desired.

Per serving: 253 calories, 6 g fat, 85 mg cholesterol, 738 mg sodium, 15.6 g carbohydrate, 2.2 g fiber, 32 g protein

Options:
- Substitute TJ's Red Thai Curry Sauce in place of Yellow Thai Curry Sauce.
- Omit pita pockets and serve over brown rice for a lower-sodium option.
- Fill sandwich (minus fresh basil and fresh spinach) and heat. Add basil and spinach before eating.
- Add 1 (15 ounce) can garbanzo beans (rinsed and drained) to add fiber.

Chicken Lime Burger with Guacamole and Salsa

Got kids? They might be able to put this meal together quickly and easily, all by themselves. It's also a great choice for after-sports or after-school snacks when dinner may still be a few hours away. Serve with low-fat tortilla chips and salsa.

Serves 4

4 TJ's frozen Chicken Lime Burgers
4 TJ's Whole Wheat Hamburger
   Buns, toasted if desired
4 tablespoons TJ's Guacamole
4 tablespoons salsa
4 leaves of lettuce
4 slices of tomato
4 slices of onion, optional

1. Heat chicken burgers according to package directions.
2. Place burgers on the bottom halves of each bun and top with the guacamole, salsa, lettuce, tomato and onion, if desired. Top with the top half of each bun.

Per serving: *285 calories, 10 g fat, 55 mg cholesterol, 607 mg sodium, 20 g carbohydrate, 5 g fiber, 24.5 g protein*

Options:
- Substitute a small slice of avocado for guacamole to reduce fat and sodium.
- Substitute TJ's Guacamole Topped with Spicy Pico De Gallo in place of guacamole and salsa.
- Serve burger atop a salad to reduce carbohydrates and sodium.

 Dairy-free

Salmon Stuffed Pitas

Did you know that most canned salmon contains wild salmon? According to the EPA (Environmental Protection Agency) we can safely consume wild salmon eight times a month as opposed to farmed salmon, which they recommend we consume only twice a month.

Take the salmon filling in a separate container and build your sandwich at lunchtime, or have this hearty sandwich for lunch or dinner at home, accompanied with soup.

Serves 4

1 (14.75 ounce) can TJ's Alaskan Pink Salmon, rinsed and drained
1 cup chopped celery
1 cup chopped, peeled cucumber (use an English cucumber if you don't want to peel it)
¼ cup TJ's Light Sour Cream
¼ cup TJ's Reduced Fat Mayonnaise
1 teaspoon dried dill
2 teaspoons TJ's 21 Seasoning Salute salt-free seasoning
½ teaspoon freshly ground black pepper
½ cup chopped green onions
4 leaves of romaine lettuce
2 TJ's Whole Wheat Pita Pockets, cut in half to make 4 pockets

In a large bowl, combine the salmon, celery, cucumber, sour cream, mayonnaise, dill, seasoning, black pepper and scallions. Chill for an hour, or longer, if possible. Serve in lettuce-lined pita pockets.

Per serving: 263 calories, 9.3 g fat, 42 mg cholesterol, 390 mg sodium, 16 g carbohydrate, 3 g fiber, 27 g protein

Options:

- Use fat free or low-fat Greek style yogurt in place of sour cream or mayonnaise to reduce fat.
- Use Italian seasoning in place of 21 Salute Seasoning for a change in flavor.
- Add sliced black olives or capers.
- Use 2 cans albacore tuna in water in place of salmon.
- Add shredded carrots, cabbage or other vegetables to increase fiber.

 *Dairy-free if use soy yogurt in place of light sour cream

Hummus and Tuna Sandwich Filling or Spread

Try this tasty alternative to tuna salad. Hummus is so much healthier than mayonnaise at 1.75 grams of fat per tablespoon versus 10 grams of fat per tablespoon for mayonnaise. Trader Joe's has a variety of hummus flavors. Experiment with this recipe to see which one you like best.

Serves 4

1 (5 ounce) can TJ's Albacore Solid White Tuna in Water, rinsed and drained
1 (7 ounce) container TJ's Spicy Hummus Dip
½ cup chopped celery or fennel
¼ cup chopped green onions
¼ teaspoon salt, optional
½ teaspoon ground cumin
⅛ teaspoon cayenne pepper
Few drops of Tabasco sauce

Combine all ingredients in a medium bowl. Use to fill a pita pocket, spread on whole wheat bread, place atop a green salad or serve as an appetizer.

Per serving: 144 calories, 6.6 g fat, 12.5 mg cholesterol, 314 mg sodium, 9.8 g carbohydrate, 2 g fiber, 10.25 g protein

Options:
- Add bottled roasted red peppers.
- Add lemon.
- Add rinsed capers.

 *Dairy-free if you use tuna without casein added (Trader Joe's does not add casein)

Asian Tuna Wraps

These sweet and crunchy wraps only take a few minutes to put together. They're ideal for lunch on the go.

Serves 6

2 (5 ounce) cans TJ's Albacore Solid White Tuna in Water, rinsed, drained and broken into chunks

¼ cup TJ's Sesame Soy Ginger Vinaigrette

¼ cup TJ's Reduced Fat Mayonnaise

1 ⅓ teaspoon TJ's Crushed Garlic or 4 cloves garlic, minced

½ teaspoon minced fresh ginger or ⅓ teaspoon bottled minced ginger

6 (8-inch) TJ's Whole Wheat Flour Tortillas

2 cups shredded bok choy (available in stocks at TJ's)

1 medium red sweet pepper, thinly sliced

½ cup jicama, cut into matchstick-size pieces

¼ cup chopped cilantro, optional

1. In a large bowl, stir together tuna, salad dressing, mayonnaise, garlic and ginger.
2. Combine bok choy, red pepper and jicama in a large bowl and toss together. Place six equal piles of the vegetable mixture onto each of the tortillas. Place the tuna filling in the middle; fold the bottom flap up and fold the sides over each other.

Per serving: *191 calories, 5.7 g fat, 16 mg cholesterol, 517 mg sodium, 31 g carbohydrate, 5.6 g fiber, 27.6 g protein*

Options:

- Use nonfat Greek style or plain yogurt in place of mayonnaise.
- Use water chestnuts in place of jicama.
- Add a few drops of TJ's Sweet Chili Sauce.
- Add slivered almonds or chopped peanuts.
- To make into a salad, eliminate the tortilla and serve the tuna atop the vegetable mixture.

 *Dairy-free if you use tuna without casein added (Trader Joe's does not add casein)

Tuna Sandwich Filling

Substituting cottage cheese for mayonnaise is an easy way to add calcium and lower fat and calories. Use as a sandwich or pita bread filling or as an appetizer on crackers, served atop a green salad or as a vegetable dip.

Serves 4

2 cups TJ's Low Fat Cottage Cheese
¼ cup sliced green onions
2 teaspoons minced parsley
4 teaspoons dried dill weed or use fresh dill, minced
4 teaspoons TJ's Reduced Sodium Soy Sauce
2 (5 ounce) cans TJ's Albacore Solid White Tuna in Water, rinsed and drained

Place cottage cheese, green onions, parsley, dill and soy sauce in a food processor or blender and blend until smooth. Add tuna and purée until smooth.

Per serving: *145 calories, 3 g fat, 182 mg cholesterol, 560 mg sodium, 4 g carbohydrate, 0 g fiber, 27 g protein*

Options:
- To lower sodium, use TJ's (5 ounce) Albacore Tuna in Water, No Salt Added or TJ's (5 ounce) Albacore Tuna in Water and Half Salt

*Gluten-free if you use tamari instead of soy sauce

Tuna, Bean and Bruschetta Salad

TJ's Bruschetta sauce adds so much flavor for so few calories. It turns Italian style vegetables into gourmet vegetables and gives a boost to homemade pizza. Here, I combine it with beans and tuna for a hearty salad. This is a great salad to take with you for lunch. Pack the lettuce leaves separately.

Serves 4

1 (5 ounce) can TJ's Albacore Solid White in Water, drained and rinsed
1 (15 ounce can) TJ's Cannellini White Kidney Beans
½ cup TJ's Bruschetta, fresh or bottled
2 green onions, chopped
¼ cup chopped basil or parsley, optional
Romaine or other lettuce leaves

Combine all of the ingredients in a medium bowl, except for the lettuce leaves. Place bean salad on lettuce leaves and serve.

Per serving: 185 calories, 2 g fat, 12.5 mg cholesterol, 576 mg sodium, 27.8 g carbohydrate, 9.5 g fiber, 14.5 g protein

Options:

- Add ½ cup chopped celery, fennel or raw zucchini.
- Add 1 (7 ounce) container of TJ's Spicy Hummus Dip.
- To lower sodium, use TJ's (5 ounce) Albacore Solid White Tuna in Water, No Salt Added, or TJ's (5 ounce) Albacore Solid White Tuna in Water and Half Salt.

*Dairy-free if you use tuna without casein added (Trader Joe's does not add casein)

Gluten-free

Savory TMT Sandwich Filling

If you can, prepare this filling a day before, to make it even more flavorful. Serve in a sandwich, on a toasted bagel or pita bread or on top of greens. Miso is a fermented Japanese paste made from soy and grain, available at health food stores and Asian markets.

Serves 6

1 (14 ounce) package TJ's Organic Firm tofu
¼ cup brown miso
⅓ cup refrigerated TJ's Tahini Sauce
2 tablespoons minced onion
½ cup minced celery
3 tablespoons unsalted sunflower seeds
3 tablespoons minced carrot, optional

Mash tofu with a fork in a medium bowl. Mix in miso and tahini. Stir in onion, seeds, and carrots, if using. Refrigerate for at least 30 minutes before using.

Per serving: 175 calories, 11.5 g fat, 0 mg cholesterol, 503 mg sodium, 7.6 g carbohydrate, 3 g fiber, 13.2 g protein

Options:
- Add balsamic vinegar.
- Add red peppers or sliced tomatoes on top of sandwich or salad.

*Gluten-free if use gluten-free miso

Vegan

Tofu, Tahini Sandwich Spread

I used to eat a tofu spread, served over greens, at The Good Earth, a popular restaurant chain. Sadly, the restaurant no longer exists, so I reconstructed this dish. Use the spread as a sandwich filling, over greens or as a vegetable dip. It's a great way to get some protein when you are on the run, as it is very portable.

Serves 4

2 cups (10 ounces) TJ's Organic Firm Tofu
2 tablespoons TJ's Tahini Sauce
2 teaspoons TJ's Reduced Sodium Soy Sauce
2-3 tablespoons minced red onions
1 tablespoon sunflower seeds, optional

Mash tofu with a fork in a medium bowl. Add the rest of the ingredients and stir together.

Per serving: 95 calories, 6.5 g fat, 0 mg cholesterol, 114 mg sodium, 2.8 g carbohydrate, 0.5 g fiber, 6.5 g protein

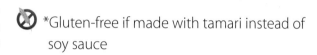 *Gluten-free if made with tamari instead of soy sauce

Vegan

Garbanzo Curry Pitas

An easy and tasty vegan sandwich with lots of fiber. Use an English cucumber if you don't want to peel it.

Serves 4

1 (15 ounce) can TJ's Garbanzo
    Beans, rinsed and drained
4 tablespoons TJ's Reduced Fat
    Mayonnaise
1 teaspoon curry powder or more
    to taste
⅛ teaspoon salt
⅛ teaspoon pepper
2 stalks of celery, diced
2 TJ's Whole Wheat Pita Pockets
½ cup peeled, sliced cucumber
Lettuce or spinach leaves
1 medium tomato, chopped,
    optional

1. In a medium bowl, roughly mash the chickpeas (garbanzo beans). Or process the chickpeas in a food processor.
2. Add mayonnaise, curry powder, salt, and pepper, and stir or process. Stir in celery.
3 Cut pitas in half and place ¼ of the filling into each half. Add the lettuce and tomato, if desired.

Per serving: *188 calories, 7.6 g fat, 0 mg cholesterol, 490 mg sodium, 29.8 g carbohydrate, 7.8 g fiber, 7.6 g protein*

Options:
- Add 1 tablespoon lemon juice, 1 clove garlic and ¼ tsp ground cumin.
- Add ¼ cup flat-leaf parsley or cilantro.
- Substitute fennel in place of celery.
- Substitute nonfat, low-fat plain yogurt, or Greek style yogurt in place of mayonnaise.
- Substitute a tortilla or wrap in place of pita pockets.

 Vegan

Veggie Hummus Wraps

Hummus is more than a vegetable dip. Try it as a sandwich filling, and experiment with all the different flavors sold at Trader Joe's to find the one you like best. You can also slice the wraps and serve them as an appetizer. Adapted from a recipe in the *PDQ Vegetarian* cookbook.

Serves 4

1 (7 ounce) container TJ's Tomato and Basil Hummus
1 (4 ounce) jar chopped pimento, rinsed and drained
4 TJ's Whole Wheat Tortillas
4 cups fresh TJ's Spinach or Wild Arugula
2 cups TJ's Shredded Carrots

Combine the hummus and pimento in a medium bowl. Spread ¼ of the mixture onto each tortilla. Add spinach and carrots and roll.

Per serving: 195 calories, 5 g fat, 0 mg cholesterol, 150 mg sodium, 40 g carbohydrate, 7.7 g fiber, 6.4 g protein

Options:

- Substitute Masala Lentil Dip in place of the hummus.
- Substitute a tortilla instead of a pita.
- Substitute roasted red peppers in place of pimentos.

*Gluten-free if you substitute TJ's Brown Rice Tortillas for whole wheat tortillas (check the label for gluten if using a different hummus)

*Vegan if you use this particular hummus (If using others, check the label for dairy ingredients)

Asparagus Veggie Sandwich

A great idea for a vegetarian sandwich, and you don't have to wait until asparagus is in season.

Serves 2

½ package (24 spears) TJ's Asparagus Spears, TJ's Grilled Asparagus Spears or fresh asparagus

2 tablespoons TJ's Reduced Fat Mayonnaise

½ teaspoon TJ's Dijon mustard

¼ loaf TJ's Focaccia, split lengthwise and in half

½ cup red pepper slices from frozen TJ's Roasted Bell Peppers and Onions

2 ounces sliced light Swiss cheese

Sliced tomatoes, optional

1½ cups baby lettuce, arugula or spinach

1. Preheat oven to 350ºF.
2. Cook asparagus according to package directions.
3. Combine mayonnaise and mustard in a small bowl.
4. Toast bread slightly in the oven.
5. Place asparagus and red peppers on two slices of the bread and cheese and tomatoes, if using, on the other two slices. Place both sides of the sandwich in the oven and bake until cheese melts, about 5 minutes.
6. Spread dressing on one side of each sandwich. Add the lettuce and close the sandwich.

Per serving: 373 calories, 8.5 g fat, 15 mg cholesterol, 775 mg sodium, 28 g carbohydrate, 3.6 g fiber, 16 g protein

Options:

- Substitute part skim mozzarella cheese for Swiss.
- Substitute TJ's Fat Free Balsamic Vinaigrette for mayonnaise.
- To lower sodium, substitute TJ's Sprouted Flourless Whole Wheat Berry Bread (160 mg sodium per slice), Sodium Free Whole Wheat Bread or other lower sodium sprouted breads at TJ's.

Lentil Tapenade Wrap

This wrap will fill you up and keep your hunger at bay for several hours due to the amount of protein and fiber in it. And it tastes good too!

Serves 2

2 TJ's Whole Wheat Tortillas
1 cup TJ's Steamed Lentils
4 tablespoons TJ's Olive Tapenade
3 tablespoons TJ's Fat Free Feta
    Cheese
1 chopped medium tomato,
    optional
¼ cup chopped red onion,
    optional
1 cup shredded lettuce

Combine lentils, tapenade and feta in a medium bowl. Place the filling in the middle of each tortilla. Add tomatoes and lettuce, and wrap the tortillas.

Per serving: *316 calories, 8.6 g fat, 1.25 mg cholesterol, 598 mg sodium, 44 g carbohydrate, 14 g fiber, 16 g protein*

Options:

- To lower sodium, cook your own lentils without salt.
- Substitute different varieties of tapenade to vary the flavor.
- Substitute arugula or spinach for lettuce.

 *Gluten-free if you substitute TJ's Brown Rice Tortillas for whole wheat tortillas

V   Vegetarian

Eggless Egg Salad

This salad is similar to the one Trader Joe's used to sell in its deli case. I took this salad to a Super Bowl party, and those who tasted it loved it and had no idea they were eating tofu and not eggs. You may be surprised, as I was, to find that Trader Joe's Reduced Fat Mayonnaise is a vegan product as well, with no eggs. This salad is great when served as a sandwich filling, spread on whole grain crackers, a side salad, a dip for endive, or when served atop a green salad.

Serves 6

1 (14 ounce) container TJ's Organic Firm Tofu
½ cup TJ's Reduced Fat Mayonnaise
2 red peppers, chopped finely
4 scallions (white and green parts), chopped finely
1 small carrot, finely shredded
3 tablespoons chopped fresh parsley
2 stalks celery, finely chopped
½ teaspoon turmeric
4 teaspoons pickle relish
1 ½ teaspoons yellow or Dijon mustard
½ teaspoon salt, optional
2 teaspoons dried dill weed
Black pepper

1. In a large bowl, mash tofu with a fork.
2. Add the remaining ingredients and mix well. Season to taste with black pepper. Refrigerate until serving.

Per serving: 133 calories, 9.3 g fat, 0 mg cholesterol, 171 mg sodium, 9.2 g carbohydrate, 6.6 g fiber, 12.3 g protein

Options:
- Add chopped black olives.
- Add celery salt to taste.
- Replace some of mayonnaise with nonfat Greek style yogurt.

*Gluten-free if you use gluten-free mustard. (Trader Joe's gluten-free mustards are Dijon, Whole Grain or Organic Yellow)

Vegan

Eggplant and Zucchini Sandwich

My recipe tasters loved this eggplant and zucchini dish over pasta. I thought it would make a great vegetarian sandwich filling too.

Serves 2

½ (8 ounce) package TJ's Grilled
    Eggplant and Zucchini Mélange
2 tablespoons TJ's Reduced Fat
    Mayonnaise
4 slices TJ's Daily Bread Sprouted
    Whole Wheat, toasted
Sliced tomatoes, optional
Sliced yellow or red onion,
    optional
Fresh basil leaves
Lettuce, spinach or arugula

1. Heat Mélange according to the
    package directions.
2. Spread the mayonnaise on each
    side of the bread and top with
    the mélange, tomato and onion,
    and if using, basil and lettuce.
    Place the toast over the lettuce
    and serve.

Per serving: 265 calories, 8.5 g fat, 5 mg cholesterol, 385 mg sodium, 37 g carbohydrate, 4.6 g fiber, 8 g protein

Options:

- Make a wrap using TJ's Whole Wheat Tortillas.
- Substitute TJ's Misto alla Griglia Eggplant and Zucchini and some mozzarella cheese in place of the mélange. Pat the vegetables with a paper towel to remove some of the olive oil before placing them on the sandwich.

 *Gluten-free if substitute brown rice bread (available at Trader Joe's) or other gluten-free bread for sprouted whole wheat bread

 Vegetarian

Chapter 7:

Easy Appetizers

For many, Trader Joe's is a favorite place to pick up easy appetizers. The following tasty recipes offer healthy and easy alternatives to higher-fat and sodium choices. Serve them at your gathering or take them to the next party you are invited to and get ready for compliments.

Polenta and Bruschetta Rounds

What a great way to use precooked polenta rounds. Slice, bake, add some Italian bruschetta and a little mozzarella and yum! This is always a big hit when I serve it.

Makes 8 rounds, serves 8

1 tube TJ's Organic Polenta
TJ's Extra Virgin Olive Oil Spray
4 tablespoons TJ's Bruschetta
   (jar or refrigerated container)
½ cup shredded part skim
   mozzarella cheese

1. Preheat oven to 350ºF.
2. Slice polenta into 8 slices and place on a baking pan sprayed with cooking spray.
3. Bake 10 minutes, remove from oven, turn the polenta over and top each round with about 1 ½ teaspoons bruschetta.
4. Top with shredded mozzarella and bake for 10 minutes, or until cheese is melted. Serve warm or cold.

Per serving (1 round): 64 calories, 1.5 g fat, 4 mg cholesterol, 271 mg sodium, 10 g carbohydrate, 0.75 g fiber, 3 g protein

Options:
Top polenta with cubed cooked chicken, fresh basil, cooked chicken sausage or cooked shrimp.

Gluten-free

Vegetarian

*Vegan if you eliminate the cheese

Curry Cheese Spread

I tasted something similar to this at a friend's gathering and reduced the fat and calories substantially. I am often asked for the recipe when I serve it.

Makes about 2 ½ cups, serves 12

1 ½ (8 ounce) containers TJ's Whipped Light Cream Cheese, or 12 ounces light or nonfat cream cheese
3 tablespoons nonfat sour cream or Greek style yogurt
⅓ cup currants
¼ cup chopped peanuts
½ cup chopped green onion
1-2 teaspoons curry powder
¼ teaspoon celery salt
½ cup TJ's Mango Ginger Chutney

1. In a medium bowl, mix together cream cheese and sour cream until soft and creamy.
2. Add the rest of the ingredients and chill until ready to serve. Spread on crackers (TJ's Raisin Rosemary Crisps would be delicious) or serve with vegetables.

Per serving *(2 tablespoons using light cream cheese):*
54 calories, 2.8 g fat, 2 mg cholesterol, 60 mg sodium, 5.2 g carbohydrate, 0 g fiber, 2 g protein

 Gluten-free

Vegetarian

*Vegan if use Tofutti Better than Cream Cheese in place of cream cheese and plain soy yogurt in place of sour cream

Blue Cheese Yogurt Dip

Adding dill makes all the difference in the flavor of this easy dip.

Makes about ¾ cup, serves 5

½ cup nonfat plain yogurt or
    Greek style yogurt
2 tablespoons crumbled
    bleu cheese
1 teaspoon lemon juice
1 clove garlic, minced
½ teaspoon balsamic vinegar
¼ teaspoon dry dill
Pinch of salt
Pinch of sugar
⅛ teaspoon freshly ground
    pepper

Combine all of the ingredients and chill for at least 30 minutes. Serve with cut-up vegetables.

Per serving (2 tablespoons): 24.2 calories, 1 g fat, 26 mg cholesterol, 64 mg sodium, 1.6 g carbohydrate, 2 g protein

 Vegetarian

Meatless Meatballs in General Tsao Sauce

You can use any meatballs but these are a great size, and are very tasty with the pineapple and stir-fry sauce. This recipe is adapted from a recipe on www.TraderJoesFan.com.

Makes 30 meatballs, serves 6

1 package TJ's Meatless Meatballs
1 cup frozen TJ's Pineapple Tidbits
    or 1 (8 ounce) can of pineapple
    tidbits
½ cup TJ's General Tsao Stir Fry
    Sauce
30 toothpicks

1. Heat the meatballs in the oven according to the package directions.
2. While they're heating, skewer one pineapple bit on the end of a toothpick.
3. Heat the sauce in a microwaveable dish for 40 seconds; remove the meatballs from oven and coat them with the heated sauce.
4. Skewer each meatball with a prepared pineapple toothpick, place on a platter, and serve.

Per serving (5 meatballs): 160 calories, 5 g fat, 0 mg cholesterol, 730 mg sodium, 18.5 g carbohydrate, 3 g fiber, 13.5 g protein

 Vegan

Lentil Pâté

Here's a great vegetarian appetizer that tastes much richer than it is.

Makes about 1 ¼ cups pâté, serves 5

1 cup TJ's Steamed Lentils
4 tablespoons TJ's Olive Tapenade
    Spread
2 ½ tablespoons TJ's Fat Free
    Crumbled Feta Cheese

Combine all of the ingredients in a food processor and blend. Serve with whole grain crackers, on sliced and toasted slices of baguette, or scooped with endive.

Per serving (¼ cup): 110 calories, 4 g fat, 0 mg cholesterol, 350 mg sodium, 11 g carbohydrate, 5 g fiber, 7 g protein

 *Gluten-free if use TJ's Artichoke Red Pepper or Green Olive Tapenade in place of Olive Tapenade Spread

 Vegetarian

Salmon Cream Cheese Spread

This recipe is from Tracy Taylor, R.D., the dietician for the cardiac rehab program we both worked with before there were any healthy shortcut products or recipes available. Our patients were so grateful for her recipes and help in learning how to cook heart-healthy recipes. She is a master at recipe development and makeovers, as you will taste for yourself here.

Makes 1 ¾ cups cup, serves 6

1 (6 ounce) can TJ's Pink Salmon, skinless, boneless, rinsed and drained

1 (8 ounce) container TJ's Light Whipped Cream Cheese

1 tablespoon chopped green onions or chives

2 teaspoons TJ's Seasoned Rice Vinegar

1 tablespoon fresh dill or 2 teaspoons dried dill weed

½ teaspoon freshly ground black pepper

Blend all of the ingredients together in a small bowl. Cover and chill until ready to serve.

Per serving (5 tablespoons): 100 calories, 6 g fat, 41 mg cholesterol, 280 mg sodium, 2.8 g carbohydrate, 9.3 g protein

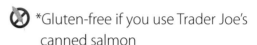 *Gluten-free if you use Trader Joe's canned salmon

Sweet Potato Hummus

Sweet, spicy and exotic at the same time, this hummus also makes a great burrito filling. To do so, add TJ's Cuban Black Beans and blend. Place in a heated tortilla with lettuce, kale or spinach. This recipe is adapted from a recipe by Debra Paquette of Restaurant Zola, in Nashville, Tenn.

Makes about 2 ¼ cups, serves 11

1 ½ (12 ounce) packages TJ's Sweet Potato Spears or Cubes (seasonal), or 1 pound sweet potatoes
1 ¼ teaspoons ground cumin
1 large lemon, juiced
¼ teaspoon cayenne pepper
⅛ teaspoon black pepper
1 tablespoon TJ's Tahini Sauce
½ tablespoon extra virgin olive oil
1 tablespoon molasses or brown sugar
Zest of one orange
¼ teaspoon dried orange peel, optional

1. Cook sweet potatoes according to package directions.
2. Add all of the ingredients to the food processor and blend until smooth and creamy.
3. Serve hummus on a bed of kale or lettuce with cut-up vegetables (cauliflower is especially delicious), or serve with toasted pita bread or pita or bagel chips.

Per serving (2 tablespoons): 56 calories, 1.2 g fat, 0 mg cholesterol, 345 mg sodium, 10.7 g carbohydrate, 1.4 g fiber, 0.81 g protein

Options:
- Use tangerine zest in place of orange zest.
- Add 1 teaspoon crumbled feta cheese.
- Use 2 teaspoons agave nectar instead of molasses.

Ⓧ Gluten-free

V Vegan

Black Bean Hummus

Here's something different that's simple to prepare with the help of a blender or food processor. It's great as a dip for jicama or other vegetables, or use it as a base for tostadas or burritos.

Beans are a wonderful source of fiber. This hummus provides over 5 grams per serving towards the recommended 25 to 30 grams per day. This recipe is adapted from a recipe that appeared in *Diabetic Meals in 30 Minutes-or Less!*

Makes about 2 cups, serves 4

1 (15 ounce) can black beans, rinsed and drained
1 tablespoon TJ's Tahini Sauce
1 tablespoon TJ's Light Sour Cream or low-fat yogurt
1 ¼ teaspoons TJ's Crushed Garlic or 4 cloves, minced
1 tablespoon minced tomato
1 tablespoon lime juice
1 teaspoon cumin
¼ cup chopped cilantro
Fresh ground pepper to taste

Combine all ingredients in a blender or food processor and process until smooth.

Per serving (1/2 cup): 116 calories, 1.3 g fat, 1.25 mg cholesterol, 277 mg sodium, 17 g carbohydrate, 5.3 g fiber, 6.5 g protein

*Diary-Free if substitute soy yogurt for sour cream or low-fat yogurt

Gluten-free

Vegetarian

Black Bean and Sweet Potato Dip

Here's a flavorful and healthy option to high-fat dips and spreads. For a burrito filling, add rice and diced mango chunks, and wrap in a tortilla. You will find a slightly different version of this dip in the vegetarian meals section for a burrito filling on page 146.

Makes about 1 ½ cups, serves 5-10

⅔ cup TJ's Sweet Potato Spears or Cubes (cubes are available seasonally)

⅔ cup canned TJ's Refried Black Beans with Jalapeño Peppers

½ cup TJ's Spicy, Smoky, Peach Salsa

1 tablespoon TJ's Sweet Chile Sauce

½ teaspoon cumin, optional

1. Cook sweet potatoes according to package directions.
2. Place sweet potatoes and refried beans in a food processor or blender and mix until blended. Stir in salsa and chili sauce. Add cumin, if using.

Serve with vegetables or baked tortilla chips.

Per serving (2 tablespoons): 33 calories, 0.8 g fat, 0 mg cholesterol, 100 mg sodium, 7 g carbohydrate, 1.2 g fiber, 1.2 g protein

Option:
Add mango chunks, diced.

 Gluten-free

Vegan

Chapter 8:

Salads, Dressings, Sauces and Dips

Tired of the same old salads? Are you ready for some inspiring and great-tasting salads, dressings, sauces and dips? Eating more salads will help you reach the goal of eating the recommended five to ten servings of vegetables and fruits per day.

Spinach and Persimmon Salad

This is one of my favorite salads to make during the holidays when persimmons are in season. Fuyus are round, hard, and a bit crunchy – perfect for salad. (Hachiyas, on the other hand, are tear-drop shaped and soft when ripe.) Trader Joe's carries all of the ingredients for this salad during the holiday season. You can prepare the dressing and persimmons up to 4 hours before assembling the salad.

Serves 12

¼ cup TJ's Seasoned Rice Vinegar
2 tablespoons orange marmalade
1 teaspoon TJ's Toasted Sesame Oil
Salt and pepper, optional
2 (12 ounce) bags TJ's Baby
    Spinach leaves or about 12 cups
    spinach leaves, rinsed and
    crisped
3 firm Fuyu persimmons (5 ounces
    each), peeled and sliced into
    thin wedges
½ cup glazed pecans, optional

1. In a large bowl, mix vinegar,
   marmalade and sesame oil. Add
   salt and pepper to taste,
   optional.
2. Add spinach, persimmons and
   pecans, if using; mix gently to
   coat with dressing.

Per serving: *85 calories, 3 g fat, 0 mg cholesterol, 107 mg sodium, 15 g carbohydrate, 3.5 g fiber, 1.3 g protein*

Options:

- Use dry roasted pecans or walnuts in place of glazed pecans.
- Use apples in place of persimmons.

 Vegan

Green Salad with Figs and Champagne Pear Vinaigrette

This is my husband's favorite salad dressing. You can substitute your favorite greens and fruit in season.

Serves 4

6 cups salad greens or
    fresh spinach
½ cup TJ's Crumbled Fat Free Feta
    Cheese (2 ounces)
4 fresh figs, quartered
2 tablespoons chopped walnuts
½ cup TJ's Champagne Pear
    Vinaigrette

Combine greens with feta, figs and walnuts. Pour salad dressing over the salad and toss.

Per serving: *122 calories, 5 g fat, 1.5 mg cholesterol, 337 mg sodium, 13 g carbohydrate, 2.68 g fiber, 6.4 g protein*

Option:
Use apples or pears instead of figs.

 Gluten-free

 Vegetarian

Carrot and Beet Salad with Arugula

This healthy, colorful and flavorful salad just happens to be super easy to put together! The recipe is adapted from one that appeared in *The Cancer-Fighting Kitchen*.

Serves 4

2 tablespoons orange juice, preferably freshly squeezed

2 teaspoons freshly squeezed lemon juice

Zest of ½ lemon, optional

2 teaspoons extra virgin olive oil

¾ teaspoon minced fresh ginger or ½ teaspoon bottled minced ginger

¼ teaspoon sea salt

1 cup TJ's Shredded Carrots

½ package (3 beets or 4 ounces) TJ's Baby Beets, sliced thinly; or use 1 cup raw shredded beets

2 cups TJ's Arugula

2 tablespoons chopped fresh mint

1. Combine orange juice, lemon juice, zest if using, olive oil, ginger and salt in a small bowl and whisk until combined.
2. Place carrots in a medium bowl. Drizzle half of the dressing over the carrots and toss until coated.
3. Add the beets and arugula. Add the rest of the dressing and toss.
4. Top with mint before serving.

Per serving: 46 calories, 2.25 g fat, 0 mg cholesterol, 32.2 mg sodium, 5.5 g carbohydrate, 1.3 g fiber, 0.8 g protein

Options:
- Add ½ cup crumbled feta cheese.
- Add ¼ cup toasted walnuts or pine nuts.

⊗ Gluten-free

🌱 Vegan

Shrimp Salad with Champagne Pear Vinaigrette

Did you know that some salad dressings will cost you 70 to 80 calories per tablespoon? Most salad bar ladles hold about 3 tablespoons each, so it is easy to add 200 to 400 extra calories to a "healthy salad." Yikes!

TJ's Champagne Pear Vinaigrette only has 22.5 calories per tablespoon. Many of my cooking class participants taste it for the first time in class and are hooked!

Serves 2

8 frozen TJ's Asparagus Spears, or use fresh asparagus
4 cups salad greens
4 ounces of (16 ounce) package frozen TJ's Cooked Medium Shrimp, Tail Off, thawed
½ pear, chopped in large chunks
2 green onions, sliced
¼ cup TJ's Champagne Pear Vinaigrette
¼ teaspoon freshly ground pepper
¼ cup TJ's Crumbled Low Fat Feta cheese, (1 ounce) optional
Chopped toasted walnuts or pecans, optional

1. Cook asparagus according to package directions and cool.
2. Place salad greens in a medium-size salad bowl and add the shrimp, pear, and onions.
3. Pour salad dressing over the salad and toss. Grind pepper on top of the salad and add feta cheese and nuts, if using.

Per serving: 133 calories, 3.65 g fat, 71 mg cholesterol, 530 mg sodium, 17 g carbohydrate, 4.65 g fiber, 16.6 g protein

Option:
Replace shrimp with crab, chicken or tofu.

Ⓧ Gluten-free

Hearts of Palm Salad

Hearts of palm are similar in texture to asparagus, minus the tips. They are low in calories and provide a slightly crunchy addition to salads. This recipe is adapted from one that appeared in *Cooking Light Super Fast Suppers*.

Serves 4

¾ ounce fresh basil leaves
  (about 12 large)
½ (14. 5 ounce) jar TJ's Hearts of
  Palm, drained and sliced
½ cup sliced bottled TJ's Fire
  Roasted Red Peppers, drained
¼ cup TJ's Fat Free Balsamic
  Vinaigrette

1. Arrange basil leaves evenly on
   4 salad plates.
2. Place hearts of palm and
   peppers over basil evenly;
   drizzle 1 tablespoon of dressing
   over each salad.

Per serving: 30 calories, 0 g fat, 0 mg cholesterol, 302 mg sodium, 6.8 g carbohydrate, 1.25 g fiber, 1.75 g protein

Ⓧ Gluten-free

V Vegan

Spinach Salad with Asian Style Spicy Peanut Vinaigrette

This is one of my favorite salads. You'll be getting 5 to 6 servings of vegetables and you won't be hungry again for a while. Love that spicy peanut vinaigrette!

Serves 2

1 (12 ounce) bag TJ's Organic
    Spinach, or 6 cups fresh spinach
10 frozen TJ's Asparagus Spears,
    cooked, or use Grilled
    Asparagus Spears or fresh
½ cup TJ's Broccoli Florets
¼ cup fresh basil leaves, chopped
Freshly ground black pepper
4 tablespoons TJ's Asian Style
    Spicy Peanut Vinaigrette
2 tablespoons vegetarian bacon
    bits, optional
Chopped peanuts, optional

1. Divide spinach between
   2 dinner-size plates.
2. Cook asparagus according to
   package directions, without oil.
3. Top spinach with vegetables
   and chopped basil. Add fresh
   pepper.
3. Pour dressing over salad and
   add vegetarian bacon bits or
   peanuts, if using.

Per serving: 102 calories, 3 g fat, 0 mg cholesterol, 228 mg sodium, 15.6 g carbohydrate, 6.3 g fiber, 7.8 g protein

Options:
- Use whatever cooked or uncooked vegetables appeal to you such as cooked green beans, cauliflower or zucchini or add avocado, bell peppers or chopped red onion.
- Add 2 tablespoons rice vinegar to the dressing so it goes further without adding fat or calories.
- Add ½ cup organic firm tofu, or TJ's Organic Baked Tofu, Teriyaki flavor, cubed, to add protein.

 Vegan

Broccoli Peanut Slaw

This crunchy, flavorful slaw combines three Trader Joe's products featuring peanuts. Peanut lovers will find it irresistible!

Serves 4

3 cups TJ's Broccoli Slaw
¼ cup TJ's Satay Peanut Sauce
1 tablespoon peanut butter, natural style, no salt added
2 tablespoons TJ's Asian Style Spicy Peanut Vinaigrette
3 green onions, chopped
4 tablespoons chopped cilantro, optional
Red pepper flakes, optional

1. Place broccoli slaw in a medium bowl.
2. Combine the satay sauce, peanut butter and vinaigrette in a small bowl and stir until blended. Add the sauce to the broccoli slaw and blend.
4. Add green onions and stir; add cilantro and red pepper flakes, if using.

Per serving: 90 calories, 5 g fat, 0 mg cholesterol, 163 mg sodium, 8.8 g carbohydrate, 2 g fiber, 3.6 g protein

Options:
- Add chopped cooked chicken, shrimp or tofu for added protein.
- Substitute chopped cabbage for part of broccoli slaw.
- Add shredded carrots and raisins.
- Use just the vinaigrette for a lighter version.

 Vegan

Orzo Spinach Salad

Here's a great summer-time salad when tomatoes and basil are in season. Orzo looks similar to rice but is actually tiny pasta which has a mild flavor and texture.

Many of my class participants have never seen or used the Dorot's frozen basil, cilantro or garlic carried by Trader Joe's until we use them in class. The packaging is bright red and is usually with the frozen vegetables. They are convenient to use in salads, soups, stews and sauces. This recipe is adapted from one that appeared in *Sunset* magazine.

Serves 12

8 ounces dry TJ's Orzo pasta
   (1 ⅓ cups)
2 cups halved cherry tomatoes
1 cup fresh basil leaves, chopped
¾ teaspoon TJ's Crushed Garlic,
   or 3 cloves garlic, minced
¼ cup TJ's Pignolia (pine nuts)
½ cup TJ's Pitted Kalamata Olives,
   halved
1 cup TJ's Fat Free Feta Cheese,
   crumbled
2 cups TJ's Baby Spinach leaves
3 tablespoons TJ's Fat Free
   Balsamic Vinaigrette
Salt and freshly ground black
   pepper

1. Cook orzo according to the package directions and rinse with cold water.
2. While pasta is cooking, combine tomatoes, basil, garlic, pine nuts, olives, feta and spinach in a large bowl.
3. Add cooked orzo; toss dressing with salad. Add salt and pepper to taste.

Per serving: 114 calories, 2.7 g fat, 1.6 mg cholesterol, 211 mg sodium, 18 g carbohydrate, 1.3 g fiber, 8.5 g protein

Option:
Use TJ's Balsamic Vinaigrette instead of the fat-free version.

 Vegetarian

Broccoli Salad with Grapes and Raisins

Our neighbor, Jane, brought a version of this salad to a neighborhood potluck. I made it lighter yet kept its great flavor.

Serves 8

2 (12 ounce) packages TJ's Broccoli Florets or 8 cups broccoli florets

1 ½ cups seedless green grapes, halved

1 cup chopped celery (2 stalks)

1 cup raisins

¼ cup salted sunflower seed kernels

⅓ cup TJ's Reduced Fat Mayonnaise or light mayonnaise

¼ cup TJ's Plain Fat Free Yogurt

1 tablespoon agave nectar or 2 tablespoons sugar

1 tablespoon white or cider vinegar

1. Combine the first 5 ingredients in a large bowl.
2. Gently whisk together mayonnaise and remaining ingredients in a small bowl.
3. Pour dressing over broccoli mixture and toss well.
4. Chill for at least 1 hour before serving.

Per serving: 160 calories, 4.3 g fat, 0.62 mg cholesterol, 10 mg sodium, 30 g carbohydrate, 3.8 g fiber, 5.3 g protein

Options:
- Substitute 2 cups cauliflower for 2 cups of the broccoli.
- Use ½ cup TJ's Greek Style 0% Nonfat Yogurt in place of mayonnaise and yogurt.
- To lower carbohydrates, use fewer grapes and/or fewer raisins.

*Dairy-Free if you substitute plain unsweetened soy yogurt for fat-free yogurt

*Gluten-free if white vinegar is distilled. Cider vinegar is gluten-free

Amazing Watermelon Greek Salad with Feta Cheese

"And now for something completely different" (for you Monty Python fans).
This is a great salad to make during the summer months when there is an abundance of watermelon, although once you taste it, you'll want it year-round. Good thing Trader Joe's carries it all year so you don't have to wait until summer.

Serves 6

¾ cup red onion, thinly sliced
1 tablespoon fresh lime juice
   (½ lime)
2 (16 ounce) packages TJ's
   Watermelon Spears or 6 cups
   seedless watermelon, cubed in
   1-inch cubes
¾ cup TJ's Crumbled Feta Cheese
½ cup sliced, pitted black olives
2 tablespoons extra virgin olive oil
1 tablespoon balsamic vinegar, or
   more to taste
Fresh parsley, chopped, for
   garnish, optional
Fresh mint, chopped, optional

1. In a small bowl, coat the onion slices with the lime juice.
2. In a large salad bowl, combine the watermelon, feta, olives and onions.
3. Whisk together the olive oil and balsamic vinegar to suit your taste and preferences. Start with 1 tablespoon and taste; add more, if desired.
4. Pour vinaigrette over melon mixture and toss. Garnish with freshly chopped parsley and/or mint, optional.

Per serving: 157 calories, 10 g fat, 7.5 mg cholesterol, 309 mg sodium, 15 g carbohydrate, 1.2 g fiber, 3.5 g protein

Options:
- Use TJ's Fat Free Feta Cheese to lower fat.
- Add white beans or cubed firm or extra firm tofu to add protein.

 *Gluten-free if use gluten-free olives (TJ's Krinos Imported Olives and Pitted Kalamata olives are gluten-free)

Black Bean Salad with Peppers and Feta Cheese

A very easy and flavorful salad. Open canned beans on the bottom of the can so that it is easier to empty them. Rinsing beans rinses away at least 1/3 the sodium.

Serves 6

2 (15 ounce) cans TJ's Black Beans, rinsed and drained
1 small each green and red bell pepper, sliced
2 green onions, minced
4 ounces TJ's Crumbled Feta Cheese
1 tablespoon extra virgin olive oil
Juice of ½ -1 lemon to taste
Freshly ground black pepper to taste, optional
Romaine lettuce

Combine all of the ingredients except the lettuce in a serving bowl; mix gently but thoroughly. Serve salad on lettuce leaves.

Per serving: *229 calories, 7 g fat, 16.8 mg cholesterol, 213 mg sodium, 30 g carbohydrate, 4.7 g fiber, 12 g protein*

Option:
Use TJ's Fat Free Feta Cheese to lower fat.

 Gluten-free

Spicy Tofu Peanut Salad

This is a remake of a very popular tofu salad sold at The Pasta Shop in Berkeley. You might want to add the curry paste gradually, tasting as you go, if you favor milder flavors. It makes a great lunch paired with stir-fried Asian-style vegetables.

Serves 3

4 tablespoons TJ's Asian Style
Spicy Peanut Vinaigrette
1 teaspoon TJ's Toasted Sesame Oil
1 teaspoon TJ's Crushed Garlic or
3 cloves garlic, minced
1 teaspoon minced fresh ginger
or ¾ teaspoon bottled minced
ginger
1 tablespoon honey
¼ teaspoon red curry paste, or
to taste
½ cup sliced green onions,
including green parts
¼ cup chopped cilantro
3 tablespoons peanut halves,
chopped
1 package TJ's Organic Baked Tofu,
Teriyaki Flavor, cubed into
1-inch cubes

1. In a medium-size bowl, mix
together vinaigrette, oil, garlic,
ginger, honey and curry paste.
2. Add onions, cilantro, peanuts
and tofu and gently combine
ingredients.

Per serving: 230 calories, 10.5 g fat, 0 mg cholesterol, 535 mg sodium, 23.5 g carbohydrate, 1.6 g fiber, 13 g protein

Options:
- Add cooked rice noodles.
- For extra flavor, add dried red pepper flakes.

Ginger Tuna Rice Salad

This is a refreshing, crunchy and sweet salad using Trader Joe's Sesame Soy Ginger Vinaigrette. It's a particularly good salad to pack for lunch.

Serves 4

1 (5 ounce) can TJ's Albacore Solid White Tuna in Water, rinsed and drained

1 pouch frozen TJ's Brown Rice or 2 cups cooked brown rice

½ cup TJ's Sesame Soy Ginger Vinaigrette

1 ½ cup frozen peas, thawed

½ cup chopped celery

6 green onions, sliced

1 cup TJ's Pineapple Tidbits, or fresh or canned pineapple

Combine all of the ingredients in a medium bowl and blend together. Serve it by itself or atop salad greens.

Per serving: 204 calories, 1.25 g fat, 12.5 mg cholesterol, 394 mg sodium, 38 g carbohydrate, 3.75 g fiber, 11.6 g protein

Options:

- Add 1 teaspoon toasted sesame oil.
- Use TJ's Biryani in place of rice.
- Use some wild rice in place of some of the brown rice.
- Use asparagus in place of peas.

 *Dairy-free if use albacore tuna without added casein (Trader Joe's does not add casein)

Roasted Red Pepper Sauce

Serve over any pasta, or gnocchi, baked potatoes, vegetables or grains. This will keep about a week stored in the refrigerator.

Makes 1 cup

⅔ cup bottled TJ's Fire Roasted
   Red Peppers, drained
⅓ cup TJ's Low Fat Buttermilk
Salt and ground black pepper

Purée red peppers and buttermilk in a blender or food processor until smooth. Add salt and pepper to taste.

Per serving *(2 tablespoons, without salt): 9 calories, 0 g fat, 0 mg cholesterol, 42 mg sodium, 0.87 g carbohydrate, 0 g fiber, 0.5 g protein*

 Gluten-free

 Vegetarian

Cilantro Yogurt Sauce

Use this sauce over burritos, tacos, tostadas, or cooked fish, or as a sandwich spread in place of mayonnaise.

Makes ¾ cup

¼ cup TJ's Cilantro Salad Dressing
½ cup TJ's Nonfat or Low Fat Plain
   Yogurt
Fresh chopped cilantro, optional

Mix ingredients in a small bowl. Add more dressing or yogurt to your taste.

Per serving *(2 tablespoons): 25 calories, 1 g fat, 0 mg cholesterol, 48 mg sodium, 1.4 g carbohydrate, 0 g fiber, 0.6 g protein*

 Vegetarian

Spicy Peanut Sauce

Use this versatile sauce as a dip for spring rolls, or as a sauce for pasta, noodles, rice or vegetables. Try it as a topping for chicken, shrimp or tofu, or as a salad dressing. This can be made a day before using and refrigerated.

Makes about 1 ¼ cups

3 tablespoons peanut butter, natural style
6 tablespoons TJ's Spicy Asian Vinaigrette
2 teaspoons TJ's Sweet Chili Sauce, optional

Combine the ingredients together and refrigerate until serving.

Per tablespoon: 56 calories, 3.4 g fat, 0 mg cholesterol, 90 mg sodium, 3.7 g carbohydrate, 0 g fiber, 1.6 g protein

 Vegan

Cranberry Mustard Sandwich Spread or Dip

Trader Joe's used to carry a similar sauce over the holiday season. I've reinvented it so I can have it on hand all year round. Spread on sandwiches or use as a baste for meats and poultry. Try it as a dip for pretzels, or spread it on a turkey or chicken slice, roll it up and serve as an appetizer.

Makes ½ cup, enough for 4 sandwiches

½ cup jellied cranberry sauce
1½ tablespoons grainy Dijon mustard
1 tablespoon brown sugar

Combine ingredients in a small mixing bowl, whisking until smooth.

Per serving (2 tablespoons): 70 calories, 0 g fat, 0 mg cholesterol, 50 mg sodium, 16 g carbohydrate, 1 g fiber, 0 g protein

Option:
Add horseradish and freshly ground black pepper to taste.

 Vegan

Really Low Fat Greek Yogurt Dressing

Here's a fresh, flavorful dressing with no leftovers to think about storing.

Makes about 4 ½ tablespoons, serves 1

2 tablespoons nonfat Greek style yogurt
½ lemon, juiced (about 2 tablespoons)
⅛ teaspoon extra virgin olive oil
¼ teaspoon Dijon mustard
¼ teaspoon sea salt
⅛ teaspoon freshly ground black pepper

Mix all ingredients together and pour over a large salad.

Per serving: *34 calories, 1 g fat, 0 mg cholesterol, 474 mg sodium, 8.3 g carbohydrate, 2.6 g fiber, 2.75 g protein*

 *Gluten-free if you use gluten-free mustard such as Trader Joe's Dijon mustard.

 Vegetarian

Dijon Dressing and Sauce

This is a simple low-calorie, low-fat salad dressing that tastes great over salads and steamed vegetables.

Makes 6 tablespoons, serves 4

1 tablespoon Dijon mustard
3 tablespoons plain nonfat yogurt
2 tablespoons balsamic vinegar

Mix ingredients well in a small bowl and pour over salad or vegetables.

Per serving (1 1/2 tablespoons): *15 calories, 0 g fat, 0 mg cholesterol, 12 mg sodium, 0 g carbohydrate, 0 g fiber, 0.5 g protein*

 *Gluten-free if you use gluten-free mustard such as Trader Joe's Dijon mustard

 Vegetarian

Horseradish-Mustard-Yogurt Sauce

Horseradish is a member of the mustard family and is a cousin to kale, cauliflower, Brussels sprouts and the common radish. Besides adding a distinctive flavor to whatever it is added or applied to, it has been prized for its medicinal and gastronomic qualities for centuries. Use this tangy sauce on turkey, chicken or fish dishes, on your favorite sandwiches or blend it into sauerkraut.

Makes 1 ½ cups, serves 24

½ cup TJ's Horseradish
½ cup Dijon mustard, or
   coarse-grained mustard
½ cup nonfat yogurt
3-5 drops Worcestershire sauce,
   optional

Combine all of the ingredients and blend; chill until ready to use. It can be stored in the refrigerator for up to 10 days.

Per serving (1 tablespoon): 8 calories, 0.2 g fat, 0 mg cholesterol, 8 mg sodium, 1.2 g carbohydrate, 0 g fiber, 0 g protein

 *Gluten-free if use Trader Joe's mustards and gluten-free Worcestershire sauce (Lea and Perrins® (made in the U.S.) and French's® brands are both gluten-free)

Chapter 9:

Hearty Soups

Trader Joe's makes preparing the following soups a snap because you start with their delicious, convenient boxed soups. Many are low in sodium, yet flavorful.

Serve low-calorie soups for lunch, with dinner, or as a snack. They can be a great way to help you get those five to ten recommended servings of vegetables and fruits per day. Since the soup bases contain no preservatives, freeze any leftover soup base you won't use in the next few days in a freezable container or freezer bag.

Weight Watcher Points™ are available online at my website: www.HealthyTraderJoes.com.

Sweet Potato-Cuban Black Bean Soup

This prepared soup is made more hearty and flavorful with the addition of beans, seasonings and salsa.

Serves 4

1 (32 ounce) box TJ's Sweet Potato
    Bisque
1 (15 ounce) can TJ's Cuban Black
    Beans, not drained
½ teaspoon ground cumin
10 drops TJ's Chili Pepper Sauce or
    other hot sauce
⅛ teaspoon cayenne pepper
2 tablespoons fresh lime juice
½ (6 ounce) container of fresh
    TJ's Salsa
2 corn tortillas, torn into pieces; or
    a few tortilla chips, optional
2 tablespoons chopped cilantro,
    optional

Combine all of the ingredients, except the corn tortillas and cilantro, in a large microwaveable bowl; stir and microwave for 3 minutes or heat in a large saucepan for 7 to 9 minutes on medium heat. Add tortillas and sprinkle with cilantro, if using.

Per serving: 232 calories, 5.25 g fat, 0 mg cholesterol, 795 mg sodium, 47 g carbohydrate, 7.6 g fiber, 7.25 g protein

Options:
- Use bottled salsa in place of fresh salsa.
- Add cubed cooked chicken or turkey sausage.

Ⓧ Gluten-free

V Vegan

Corn and Soycutash Soup

It's amazing what you can come up with when rummaging through the freezer and pantry. This soup makes a meal starter or an entrée when served with salad and crusty bread.

Serves 4

3 cups TJ's Creamy Corn and
   Red Pepper Soup
1 cup TJ's Organic Low Sodium
   Chicken Broth
2 cups frozen TJ's Soycutash
½ pound frozen TJ's Medium
   Cooked Shrimp, Tail Off, thawed
   and rinsed
¼ cup refrigerated TJ's Cilantro
   Salad Dressing
Freshly ground black pepper
2 tablespoons chopped cilantro,
   optional

Combine all of the ingredients except cilantro, if using, in a large microwaveable bowl, stir, and microwave 3 to 4 minutes. Or heat in a large saucepan on medium heat 8 to 10 minutes, until the soup is heated through. Sprinkle with cilantro, if using, and serve.

Per serving: 268 calories, 7.4 g fat, 73 mg cholesterol, 851 mg sodium, 29 g carbohydrate, 6.5 g fiber, 20 g protein

Option:
Replace shrimp with cooked chicken sausage.

Butternut Squash-Curry and Peanut Butter Soup

Butternut squash soup makes a great base for lots of flavorful soups. Here, I've added peanut butter and a few Indian spices.

Serves 6

1 ½ (32 ounce) boxes TJ's Butternut Squash Soup

3 tablespoons peanut butter, natural style

3 teaspoons turmeric

3 teaspoons garam masala or curry powder

1 teaspoon nutmeg, preferably freshly ground

3 tablespoons chopped cilantro, optional

Place all of the ingredients, except cilantro, in a microwavable bowl and stir. Microwave for 3 to 4 minutes or heat in a large saucepan on medium heat 8 to 10 minutes or until the soup is warm. Top with cilantro, if using.

Per serving: 137 calories, 6.3 g fat, 0 mg cholesterol, 593 mg sodium, 17 g carbohydrate, 3.6 g fiber, 4 g protein

Options:

- Add firm tofu, cut into small cubes to add protein.
- Use TJ's Organic Low Sodium Butternut Squash to lower sodium to 108 mg sodium per serving.
- Add brown rice to thicken soup.
- Add cooked butternut squash cubes.

 Gluten-free

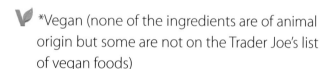 *Vegan (none of the ingredients are of animal origin but some are not on the Trader Joe's list of vegan foods)

Turkey Meatball Wild Rice Soup

I've combined Trader Joe's turkey meatballs with chicken broth, cooked wild rice and a few other ingredients to create this delicious soup. Precook the wild rice or bring some out of the freezer that you have previously frozen to serve this within minutes.

Serves 4

¾ cup TJ's Wild Rice, uncooked
1 box (32 ounces) TJ's Organic Low Sodium Chicken Broth
8 frozen TJ's Turkey Meatballs, thawed and quartered
2 cups sliced mushrooms
1 cup TJ's Shredded Carrots
1 teaspoon poultry seasoning
2 tablespoons dry sherry
1 cup low-fat milk
2 tablespoons fresh parsley, optional
2 tablespoons bacon bits, optional
2 tablespoons cornstarch
¼ cup water

1. Cook wild rice according to package directions.
2. While wild rice is cooking, combine chicken broth, meatballs, mushrooms and carrots in a saucepan.
3. Add poultry seasoning, sherry, milk, cooked wild rice and pepper.
4. Place the cornstartch in a cup or small bowl and add the water; mix with a fork or whisk to dissolve cornstarch. Add the mixture to the soup and stir until soup is thickened, about 5 minutes. If a thicker soup is desired, add more cornstarch using the same method as above.

Per serving: *300 calories, 5 g fat, 33 mg cholesterol, 523 mg sodium, 41 g carbohydrate, 7.3 g fiber, 24 g protein*

Sassy Black Bean Soup

Peach salsa is the magic ingredient in this tasty soup. Use the leftover salsa in bean dips, on chicken or fish or even mixed with tofu and rice.

Serves 4

1 box (32 ounces) TJ's Latin Black Bean Soup

½ pouch frozen TJ's Brown Rice or 1 cup cooked brown rice

1 cup TJ's Smoky, Spicy, Peach Salsa

2 tablespoons chopped cilantro, optional

Combine the soup, brown rice and salsa in a large microwavable bowl, stir, and heat for 4 minutes or heat in a saucepan on medium heat for 7 to 8 minutes. Sprinkle with cilantro, if desired.

Per serving: *160 calories, 25 g fat, 0 mg cholesterol, 700 mg sodium, 21.5 g carbohydrate, 5 g fiber, 5 g protein*

Options:

- Add black beans, cubed cooked chicken or tofu.
- Top with plain non or low-fat yogurt.

 Gluten-free

Vegan

Latin Black Bean Soup with Pumpkin

Pumpkin is a low-calorie vegetable (26 calories per 3 ounces) and is a good source of fiber, antioxidants, vitamins and minerals. It also tastes great combined with black beans. I use it as a substitute for oil when I make brownies from a box (you can't taste the difference and you save almost 6 grams of fat per serving) and have added it to waffle and pancake batter as well as used it when making muffins. Canned pumpkin is available at Trader Joe's seasonally.

Serves 2

2 cups TJ's Latin Black Bean Soup
1 cup canned pumpkin
4 tablespoons TJ's Spicy, Smoky, Peach Salsa
¼ cup chopped cilantro, optional

Add soup, pumpkin and peach salsa in a microwaveable bowl and stir. Heat for 3 minutes or heat in a saucepan over medium heat for 7 to 8 minutes. Sprinkle with cilantro if desired.

Per serving: *125 calories, 1.5 g fat, 0 mg cholesterol, 615 mg sodium, 23 g carbohydrate, 9 g fiber. 6 g protein*

Options:
- Add brown rice.
- Add diced zucchini.
- Add TJ's Spicy Jalapeño Chicken Sausage.
- Add tuna or cooked chicken or tofu.
- Add a few drops of hot sauce.

 Gluten-free

 Vegan

Hummus Soup

Trader Joe's White Bean and Basil Hummus is my favorite variety. I use it to make this simple soup in minutes. It will give you 4.75 grams of fiber to contribute to your recommended 25 to 30 grams per day.

Serves 4

3 ½ cups TJ's Organic Low Sodium Vegetable Broth
1 ½ cups TJ's White Bean and Basil Hummus
1 (15 ounce) can TJ's Cannellini White Kidney Beans, Northern white beans, or Navy beans
8 fresh basil leaves, chopped

Combine all ingredients except basil in a microwavable bowl and stir. Heat for about 4 minutes or heat soup for about 7 minutes in a large saucepan over medium-high heat. Garnish with basil leaves.

Per serving: *200 calories, 5 g fat, 0 mg cholesterol, 460 mg sodium, 24 g carbohydrate, 4.75 g fiber, 4.5 g protein*

Options:

• Add cooked sausage, chicken or tofu to soup.
• Use other flavors of hummus and use garbanzo beans instead of cannellini beans.
• Use flat-leaf parsley instead of basil.
• Add 1 to 2 teaspoons of lemon juice.

V Vegetarian

Tzatziki Soup

This is a cold soup. I tell you that because I was on a date many years ago and ordered gazpacho. I took one sip and exclaimed that it was cold. My date looked at me like I was from another planet and then calmly explained that it was supposed to be cold. Was I embarrassed? Just a bit.

Serves 3-4

1 (12 ounce) container TJ's Tzatziki
1 cup TJ's Low Fat Buttermilk
½ teaspoon dried dill weed or
   2 teaspoons chopped fresh dill
Chopped tomatoes, optional
A few sprigs fresh dill for garnish,
   optional

Combine all of the ingredients in a medium bowl or large measuring cup and stir. Pour into four bowls. Add chopped tomatoes and fresh dill, if using.

Per serving: *145 calories, 8.5 g fat, 20 mg cholesterol, 155 mg sodium, 12 g carbohydrate, 0 g fiber, 7 g protein*

 Vegetarian

Roasted Red Pepper and Lentil Soup

Lentils come already steamed at Trader Joe's and are a wonderful source of protein. Add them to soups and salads or serve as an entrée mixed with one of TJ's simmer sauces or salsas.

Serves 4

1 box (32 ounces) TJ's Tomato & Roasted Red Pepper Soup
1 ½ cups TJ's Steamed Lentils
1 teaspoon cumin

Per serving: 145 calories, 3.5 g fat, 10 mg cholesterol, 230 mg sodium, 22.5 g carbohydrate, 5 g fiber, 5.3 g protein

Options:

- Add cooked cut-up sweet potato or butternut squash.
- Substitute white beans in place of lentils.

 Gluten-free

 Vegan

Spinach Tortellini Soup

Combine packaged tortellini and frozen spinach in chicken broth for this quick and easy soup. Despite using packaged products, the sodium level is low.

Serves 6

1 ½ boxes (6 cups) TJ's Organic Low Sodium Chicken Broth

1 (10 ounce) package fresh TJ's Cheese Tortellini

½ package (8 ounces) frozen TJ's Spinach, thawed and squeezed; or 8 ounces fresh spinach

⅓ to ½ teaspoon TJ's Crushed Garlic or 1-2 cloves, minced

¼ cup fresh basil, finely chopped; or 1 tablespoon dried basil leaves

½ teaspoon dried oregano leaves

1 (14.5 ounce) can TJ's Organic Diced & No Salt Added Tomatoes

Freshly ground pepper

¼ cup freshly grated Parmesan cheese

1. In a large pot, bring the chicken broth to a simmer over medium-high heat.
2. Stir in the tortellini, lower the heat and simmer gently for 3 minutes.
3. Stir in the spinach, garlic, oregano, tomatoes and pepper. Return to a simmer and cook for 2 to 3 more minutes and add fresh basil. (If using dried basil, add it with the spinach, etc.) Serve hot and sprinkle with Parmesan cheese.

Per serving: 174 calories, 3.4 g fat, 20 mg cholesterol, 238 mg sodium, 29 g carbohydrate, 5.25 g fiber, 10.5 g protein

Options:

- Sauté 1 chopped onion for 5 minutes before adding chicken broth in step 1.
- Substitute 1 or 2 Dorot frozen cubes of basil for fresh or dried basil.
- Add diced chicken.

Susan's Roasted Red Pepper Soup

Susan sometimes works the demo station at my local Trader Joe's. She shared this recipe she developed. Customers love it (along with Susan's incredible laugh) and so does everyone I serve it to.

Serves 4

1 box (32 ounces) TJ's Organic Low Sodium Tomato & Roasted Red Pepper Soup

1 (13.75 ounce) jar TJ's Corn and Chile Tomato-Less Salsa

1 (15 ounce) can TJ's Black Beans, rinsed and drained

Combine all of the ingredients and heat in a large microwavable bowl for 3 to 4 minutes or heat in a saucepan on medium heat for 8 to 10 minutes.

Per serving: *311 calories, 3.5 g fat, 10 mg cholesterol, 657 mg sodium, 59 g carbohydrates, 6.8 g fiber, 11 g protein*

Options:

- Add 1 cup cooked brown rice.
- Add 1 cup cooked chicken.
- Add 1 or 2 chopped TJ's Spicy Jalapeño Chicken Sausages.

Gluten-free

Vegan

Chapter 10:

Chicken Entrées

Most of these quick recipes use cooked chicken in the form of Trader Joe's Just Chicken or the frozen version, Just Grilled Chicken Strips. The frozen version is great for when you want to use just a few pieces. You can reseal the bag and put it back in the freezer. The frozen strips have 40 mg more sodium per 3 ounces. You can also freeze Just Chicken, if you will not be able to use all of the 16 ounces within a couple of days. As in all of the entrée chapters, I have included serving suggestions along with calorie counts, if appropriate, for those of you counting calories.

You can find more entrée recipes in my previous book, *Quick and Healthy Meals from Trader Joe's*, available on my website www.HealthyTraderJoes.com, online at Amazon, and at select Barnes and Nobles bookstores.

Weight Watcher Points™ are available online at my website: www.HealthyTraderJoes.com.

Chicken Salad with Raspberries

Sometimes it's just too hot to cook. This recipe is for days like those, as well as days you just want something different and flavorful.

Serves 4

12 ounces (¾ package) TJ's Just Chicken; frozen TJ's Just Grilled Chicken Strips, defrosted; or cooked chicken breast
8 cups TJ's Baby Spinach or mixed salad greens
½ cup TJ's Raspberry Vinaigrette
1 cup raspberries

Slice cooked chicken into bite-size pieces and place in a large bowl. Add salad greens and vinaigrette and toss. Sprinkle raspberries on top.

Per serving: *236 calories, 5.75 g fat, 198 mg cholesterol, 407 mg sodium, 12.8 g carbohydrate, 3.25 g fiber, 31.5 g protein*

 Dairy-free

Serve with:
Quick and Super-quick: Tzatziki Soup, (145 calories/serving) page 100

Chicken à la King with Asparagus

Smooth and creamy with the addition of asparagus, this childhood dish for many is remade with much lighter ingredients. Adapted from a recipe from the American Heart Association.

Serves 4

TJ's Extra Virgin Olive Oil Spray

⅓ teaspoon TJ's Crushed Garlic, or 1 clove, minced

¾ package (8 ounces) frozen TJ's Asparagus Spears, cut on the bias in bite-size pieces, or use fresh

1 (12 ounce) can fat-free evaporated milk

⅓ cup all-purpose flour

2 tablespoons dry sherry

2 cups (8 ounces) TJ's Just Chicken or 2 cups chopped cooked chicken breast

2 cups frozen TJ's Fire Roasted Bell Peppers and Onions

Salt and pepper

2 pouches frozen TJ's Brown Rice, heated; or 4 cups cooked brown rice

1. In a large nonstick skillet sprayed with olive oil spray, add garlic, asparagus, broth, and thyme and cook over high heat. Bring to a boil and then reduce the heat and simmer, covered, for 5 minutes.
2. Whisk together the flour and half of the evaporated milk in a medium bowl. Stir it into the asparagus broth. Add the remaining evaporated milk and cook for 10 minutes longer, or until thickened, stirring occasionally.
3. Add sherry, chicken, bell peppers and onions and cook for 2 more minutes, stirring constantly. Season to taste with salt and pepper, if desired. Serve over warm brown rice.

Per serving: 353 calories, 2.8 g fat, 43 mg cholesterol, 238 mg sodium, 54 g carbohydrate, 5 g fiber, 24.5 g protein

Options:
- Substitute tarragon in place of thyme.
- Add ½ to 1 teaspoon nutmeg.
- Serve over whole wheat noodles or whole wheat bread instead of rice.

Serve with:
Quick: Green Salad with Figs and Champagne Pear Vinaigrette (122 calories/serving), page 76
Super-quick: TJ's Organic Low Sodium Roasted Red Pepper and Lentil Soup (110 calories/cup), page 101

Cranberry Chicken Wild Rice Salad

Cranberries aren't just for the holidays anymore, and they have many health benefits if eaten on a regular basis. You can enjoy this delicious main meal salad all year long, quickly and easily with convenient cooked chicken, cranberries and Cranberry, Walnut and Gorgonzola Salad Dressing from Trader Joe's. Precook the wild rice or bring some out of the freezer that you have previously frozen. It freezes well.

Serves 4

½ cup TJ's Wild Rice, uncooked
½ (8 ounce) package TJ's Just Chicken, or cooked chicken or turkey breast, cut into bite-size pieces
½ cup TJ's Dried Cranberries
2 green onions, sliced
1 stalk celery, sliced
6 tablespoons refrigerated TJ's Cranberry, Walnut and Gorgonzola Salad Dressing
4 lettuce leaves

1. Cook wild rice according to package directions.
2. Combine wild rice, chicken, cranberries, green onions and celery in a medium bowl.
3. Drizzle dressing over salad and toss. Spoon evenly onto four lettuce leaves.

Per serving: 263 calories, 5 g fat, 43 mg cholesterol, 160 mg sodium, 36.5 g carbohydrate, 2.8 g fiber, 20 g protein

Option:
Sprinkle toasted walnuts or pecans over salad before serving.

 Gluten-free

Serve with:
Quick and Super-quick: Hummus Soup (200 calories/serving), page 99

Thai Chicken Pizza

I could eat Trader Joe's Satay Peanut Sauce with a spoon, all by itself (which I admit I sometimes do) - it's that good! I've used it here in what may seem like an unusual combination but it works. The cooking directions for the pizza shell are different from those on the package and can be used for any type of pizza you might make from TJ's pizza dough. The sodium is a bit high in this recipe, so balance out the day with lower sodium breakfast and lunch choices. From my *Quick and Healthy Meals from Trader Joe's* cookbook.

Serves 4

TJ's Extra Virgin Olive Oil Spray
1 bag TJ's Wheat Pizza Dough, or
    prepared pizza crust
7 ounces TJ's Satay Peanut Sauce
4 ounces TJ's Just Chicken,
    cut into strips
½ cup shredded part skim
    mozzarella
1 bunch green onions, chopped
½ cup fresh bean sprouts
½ cup shredded carrots
1 tablespoon chopped roasted
    peanuts, optional
¼ cup chopped cilantro, optional

1. Place the oven rack on the lowest rung and preheat the oven to 450ºF. Let the dough rest on the counter for 20 minutes.
2. Spray a cookie sheet with olive oil spray, avoiding the edges so the dough will stick when the dough is spread to the edges. Put a little olive oil on your hands or spray with olive oil spray and form the pizza dough into a circle the diameter of your pizza pan. Place it on the pan, patting it with your oiled hands until the dough is evenly spread and reaches the edge of the pan.
3. Bake the dough for 10 minutes or until it is slightly brown. Cool 5 minutes and add the satay sauce, chicken and cheese. Place the pizza on the top shelf of the oven and bake 8 to 12 minutes.
4. Add onions, bean sprouts, carrots, peanuts and cilantro, if desired. Slice into 4 wedges.

Per serving: 380 calories, 12 g fat, 36 mg cholesterol, 893 mg sodium, 57 g carbohydrate, 6 g fiber, 21 g protein

Serve with:
Quick and Super-quick: TJ's Broccoli Slaw with Spicy Asian Peanut Vinaigrette

Pumpkin Chicken Enchiladas

Pumpkin is high in vitamin C and beta carotene and low in carbohydrates and calories. Plus, it has zero cholesterol. The blending of pumpkin and black beans makes for a flavorful, healthy and filling combination. Adapted from *Martha Stewart's Everyday Food* cookbook.

Serves 4

2 cups (8 ounces) frozen TJ's Just Grilled Chicken Strips, thawed; or 2 cups cooked chicken, shredded

1 cup canned TJ's Black Beans, rinsed and drained

6 green onions, thinly sliced

¼ cup chopped cilantro

¼ teaspoon freshly ground pepper

1 (15 ounce) can pumpkin

1 ⅓ teaspoons TJ's Crushed Garlic or 4 cloves, minced

1 chipotle chili in 1 tablespoon adobo sauce or 1 jalapeño chili, quartered (remove ribs and seeds if you want less heat)

1 teaspoon chili powder

½ teaspoon cumin

2 ½ cups TJ's Organic Low Sodium Chicken Broth

TJ's Extra Virgin Olive Oil Spray

8 TJ's Corn Tortillas

6 slices TJ's Light White Cheddar cheese

1. Preheat oven to 425°F.
2. In a medium bowl, combine chicken, scallions and cilantro. Season with pepper.
3. Purée pumpkin, garlic, chili and adobo, chili powder, cumin and chicken broth in a blender or food processor until smooth.
4. Spray an 8 or 9-inch square baking pan with vegetable spray. Pour 1 cup of pumpkin sauce in the bottom of the pan.
5. Divide the chicken evenly between the tortillas. Roll up tortillas and lay them seam-side down in the baking pan.
6. Pour the remaining pumpkin sauce on top. Lay cheese slices evenly on top. Place the dish on a baking sheet to catch drips. Bake until cheese is golden and sauce is bubbling, 25 to 30 minutes. Let cool 5 minutes before serving.

Per serving: 377 calories, 9.8 g fat, 65 mg cholesterol, 752 mg sodium, 53 g carbohydrate, 14 g fiber, 35 g protein

Option:
Substitute cooked sweet potatoes for canned pumpkin purée.

Serve with:
Quick and Super-quick: Green salad with TJ's Cilantro Salad Dressing and heated corn or whole wheat flour tortillas

Italian Sausage and Beans over Polenta

Here's a gluten-free way to serve hearty Italian food. Beans add a good source of fiber and some protein. When you are using reduced sodium products (in this case, Organic Marinara-No Salt Added), it's a good idea to add extra herbs and salt-free seasonings to enhance the flavor.

Serves 8

TJ's Extra Virgin Olive Oil Spray
1 round of TJ's Organic Polenta
⅔ teaspoon TJ's Crushed garlic or
   2 garlic cloves, minced
½ onion, diced
1 red pepper, chopped
1 zucchini, chopped
1 ½ cups TJ's Organic Marinara -
   No Salt Added
½ teaspoon dried oregano
½ teaspoon dried basil
1 (12 ounce) package TJ's Spicy
   Italian Chicken Sausage
1 (15 ounce) can TJ's Cannellini
   Beans, rinsed and drained
6 TJ's Pitted Kalamata olives, sliced
2 tablespoons flat-leaf parsley,
   chopped
¼ cup shredded Parmesan
   cheese

1. Preheat oven to 400ºF. Spray a baking sheet with oil spray. Slice polenta into 10 to 12 slices and place on the baking sheet. Bake for 5 minutes each side. Place polenta on a large plate or serving dish.
2. Add 2 tablespoons of water to a skillet on medium-high heat. Add garlic, onion, bell pepper and zucchini and cook for 3 to 4 minutes. Add marinara, oregano and basil and simmer for 5 minutes.
3. Add sausage, beans, olives and parsley and stir. Cook until sausage and beans are heated through.
4. Spoon sausage and sauce over the polenta and top with the Parmesan cheese.

Per serving: 217 calories, 6 g fat, 30 mg cholesterol, 650 mg sodium, 25 g carbohydrate, 6.7 g fiber, 16 g protein

Options:
- Grill polenta instead of baking it.
- Serve sauce over pasta, rice or quinoa instead of polenta.

 Gluten-free

Serve with:
Quick: Hearts of Palm Salad (30 calories/serving), page 79
Super-quick: Fresh spinach salad with Fat Free Balsamic Vinaigrette, or fresh lemon and lime juice drizzled over the spinach

Naan Pizzas with Pesto

I adapted this recipe from one in *Sunset* magazine. The original version had 942 calories, 69 grams of fat and 1776 mg of sodium per serving! My recipe tasters thought this version was very flavorful, even though it is so much lower in calories, fat, and sodium. By using the whole wheat version of the naan, you are adding more fiber to your diet.

Serves 4

½ cup slivered red onion

2 tablespoons TJ's Fat Free
  Balsamic Vinaigrette

4 TJ's Whole Wheat Naan Breads
  (3 ounces each)

4 tablespoons fresh TJ's Pesto

1 link TJ's Spicy Italian Chicken
  Sausage, sliced thinly

¼ cup diced roasted red peppers

8 pitted kalamata olives

2 tablespoons fresh basil, chopped

¼ cup grated Romano cheese or
  Parmesan cheese

2 cups lightly packed TJ's Baby
  Spinach or Wild Arugula,
  chopped

1. Preheat over to 400ºF.
2. Combine onion and vinaigrette, set aside.
3. Place naan on baking sheet and bake about 5 minutes.
4. Spread each naan with 1 tablespoon pesto then arrange sausage, peppers, olives, basil and a layer of cheese evenly on the naan. Bake until cheese softens - about 5 minutes.
5. Add spinach to onion and vinaigrette mixture.
6. Toss to coat and arrange over pizzas. Serve warm.

Per serving: 382 calories, 13 g fat, 22 mg cholesterol, 480 mg sodium, 46 g carbohydrate, 9 g fiber, 18 g protein

Options:
- Serve greens separately, as a salad.
- Substitute garlic-flavored naan, pita bread or flatbread for the whole wheat naan.

Serve with:
Quick: Lemony Asparagus with Parsley (45 calories/serving), page 164
Super-quick: Grilled Eggplant and Zucchini Mélange (70 calories/serving)

Mexican Chicken Stew

The key to adding lots of flavor to this quick dish, without adding lots of salt, is the addition of jalapeño, lime juice and cilantro. I also used TJ's Diced & No Salt Added Tomatoes to cut down on sodium.

Serves 4 to 6

1 medium onion, diced, or 1 cup TJ's Diced Onions

⅔ teaspoon TJ's Crushed Garlic or 2 garlic cloves, finely chopped

1 jalapeño pepper, seeds and stem removed and finely chopped

1 tablespoon water

3 cups (12 ounces) TJ's Just Chicken, or 3 cups cooked chicken, shredded

½ (1.25 ounce) package TJ's Taco Seasoning Mix

2 (14.5 ounce) cans TJ's Diced & No Salt Added Tomatoes, undrained

1 (15 ounce) can TJ's Black Beans, drained and rinsed

1 cup frozen TJ's Corn

1 cup TJ's Organic Low Sodium Chicken Broth

2 tablespoons fresh lime juice, optional

¼ cup chopped cilantro, optional

1. Cook onion, garlic and jalapeño in water in a large pot until tender, about 3 minutes.
2. Add cooked chicken, taco seasoning, tomatoes, beans and corn.
3. Bring to a boil; reduce heat and simmer 15 minutes, stirring occasionally.
4. Serve garnished with lime juice and cilantro, if desired.

Per serving: 294 calories, 1.8 g fat, 48 mg cholesterol, 503 mg sodium, 40 g carbohydrate, 12.8 g fiber, 26 g protein

Options:
- Add 2 cups brown or white rice.
- Top with grated pepper jack cheese, low-fat cheese, or avocado slices.
- For a vegetarian version, use 2 cans of beans and eliminate chicken.
- Add 1 teaspoon cumin or chili powder for added flavor.
- Add 2 teaspoons of cornstarch (mixed with some of broth before adding) after step 2 to thicken the stew.
- Top each serving with a dollop of nonfat yogurt or low-fat sour cream.

Dairy-free

*Gluten-free if you use TJ's Organic Low Sodium Chicken Broth or TJ's Organic Free Range Chicken Broth. Both are on Trader Joe's "No Gluten" list.

Serve with:

Quick: TJ's Cornbread (290 calories and 12.5 g fat if you follow directions on the box and use the oil). If made with unsweetened applesauce in place of oil, it is only 190 calories/serving and 0.5 g fat. Save 100 calories and 12 grams of fat by making this substitution. You can use applesauce in place of the oil when you make it from scratch as well. Substitute frozen apple juice concentrate, stevia or agave nectar for sugar when making from scratch. (This cornbread mix is very sweet, almost like cake; you might want to make it from a recipe that uses less sugar.)

Super-Quick:

Green salad with TJ's Cilantro Salad Dressing

Tropical Chicken and Rice

I was playing with some ingredients I had on hand in the kitchen one evening, tasting as I went along, and came up with this sweet tropical combination. I love it when that happens! Bananas and pineapple add sweetness that blend well with the peppers, chiles and cardamom.

Serves 4

2 tablespoons water or TJ's Organic Low Sodium Chicken Broth

1 medium onion, chopped, or 1 cup TJ's Diced Onions

1 cup frozen TJ's Mélange à Trios (bell peppers) or Fire Roasted Bell Peppers and Onions

2 tablespoons canned TJ's Fire Roasted Green Chiles

2 firm, ripe medium bananas

½ cup frozen TJ's Pineapple Tidbits

¾ cup orange juice

¼ cup fresh lime juice

1 cup TJ's Black Beans, drained and rinsed

1 teaspoon cardamom

½ package (8 ounces) TJ's Just Chicken or 2 cups cooked chicken

1 pouch frozen TJ's Brown Rice or 2 cups cooked brown rice

¼ cup fresh chopped cilantro, optional

1. Heat water in a large nonstick skillet on medium-high heat. Add onions and cook until translucent, about 3 minutes.
2. Add the rest of the ingredients and simmer 5 to 7 minutes or until warm. Top with cilantro, if desired.

Per serving: 320 calories, 2.2 g fat, 43 mg cholesterol, 190 mg sodium, 52 g carbohydrate, 7 g fiber, 22.5 g protein

Options:
- Use TJ's Lemon Pepper Chicken strips or fresh or frozen grilled chicken in place of Just Chicken.
- Top with unsweetened coconut.

 Dairy-free

 *Gluten-free (Fire Roasted Green Chiles was not on the "No Gluten" list for Trader Joe's but it may be gluten-free. If not, substitute fresh jalapeño or other chili peppers.)

Serve with:
Quick and Super-quick: Green salad with 2 tablespoons TJ's Champagne Pear Vinaigrette and fresh or canned pineapple slices (30 calories each ring)

Simple Asian Chicken Stir-Fry

Preparing quick meals using Trader Joe's fresh Asian Stir Fry Vegetables makes it super convenient to get in the recommended five to ten servings of vegetables and fruits per day, a priority if you want to lose weight and stay light and healthy.

Serves 4

½ cup TJ's Free Range Chicken Broth

1 teaspoon fresh grated ginger or ⅔ teaspoon bottled minced ginger

⅓ teaspoon TJ's Crushed Garlic or 1 clove garlic, minced

1 container TJ's Asian Stir Fry Vegetables

2 cups (8 ounces) TJ's Just Chicken or 2 cups cooked chicken, shredded

¼ cup TJ's General Tsao Stir Fry Sauce

1 pouch frozen TJ's Brown Rice, or 2 cups cooked brown rice

Cilantro, optional

1. Heat chicken broth in a large nonstick skillet over medium-high heat. Add ginger and garlic and cook for 2 minutes, stirring constantly. Add the Asian Stir Fry Vegetables and cook for about 7 minutes, stirring frequently. Add chicken, cover and let simmer for 3 to 4 minutes.
2. Meanwhile, heat rice according to package directions.
3. Add stir-fry sauce and stir to combine. Serve the chicken stir-fry over rice and top with cilantro, if desired.

Per serving: 225 calories, 2 g fat, 43 mg cholesterol, 313 mg sodium, 35 g carbohydrate, 3.75 g fiber, 20 g protein

Options:
- Use TJ's Soyaki instead of General Tsao sauce.
- Use TJ's Asian Style Spicy Peanut Vinaigrette or Satay Peanut Sauce in place of General Tsao sauce.
- Replace fresh vegetables with frozen TJ's Stir Fry Vegetables.

 Dairy-free

Serve with:
Quick: Broccoli with Lemon Zest (38 calories/serving), page 165
Super-quick: Steamed fresh or frozen broccoli sprinkled with TJ's Sesame Soy Ginger Vinaigrette

Italian Chicken Pasta with Feta

Orzo looks very similar to rice, but it's actually small rice-shaped pasta. The combination of pasta, pre-cooked chicken, Italian sauce and feta makes a delicious gourmet meal in just minutes.

Serves 4

1 cup dry TJ's Orzo Pasta

⅓ cup TJ's Chicken Broth

1 ½ medium onions or 1 ½ cups TJ's Diced Onions

½ teaspoon TJ's Crushed Garlic, or 1 large clove, minced

1 ¾ cups TJ's Organic Marinara with No Salt Added

8 ounces TJ's Just Chicken or 2 cups cooked chicken breast

1 teaspoon sugar, optional

2 tablespoons wine vinegar

½ cup TJ's Reduced Fat Crumbled Feta

¼ cup fresh chopped or snipped basil

1. Cook orzo pasta according to package directions. Drain and keep warm.
2. While pasta is cooking, heat broth in a large nonstick skillet and cook onions and garlic, stirring often until onions are translucent, about 3 minutes.
3. Add marinara, chicken and sugar, if using, and stir to combine. Simmer for 5 minutes.
4. Add vinegar, orzo and feta and stir until combined. Serve topped with chopped basil.

Per serving: *322 calories, 4 g fat, 48 g cholesterol, 283 mg sodium, 44 g carbohydrate, 3.7 g fiber, 25 g protein*

Options:
- Substitute your favorite whole wheat pasta or brown rice for the orzo to increase fiber.
- Use any of Trader Joe's marinara sauces, with the understanding that the amount of sodium per serving will likely be higher.
- Add dried Italian seasonings to taste.
- Use TJ's Fat Free Crumbled Feta to further reduce fat and cholesterol.

Serve with:
Quick: Lemony Asparagus with Parsley (45 calories/serving), page 164
Super-quick: TJ's Bean so Green (90 calories/serving)

Braised Chicken Sausage and Apples

Trader Joe's chicken sausages have a third or less fat than traditionally prepared sausages and still taste great. I tend to think of sausages as "guy" food, and add them to soups and lighter meals for my husband and sons, who appreciate the addition.

Serves 4

2 tablespoons water
1 chopped onion or 1 cup refrigerated TJ's Diced Onions
2 medium Fuji, Pippin or Granny Smith apples, peeled and thinly sliced
6 tablespoons Chardonnay
1 ⅓ cups TJ's Organic Low Sodium Chicken Broth
¾ teaspoon dried thyme
¾ teaspoon nutmeg
1 package TJ's Smoked, Apple Chardonnay Chicken Sausage, cut into 1-inch slices
4 medium potatoes (2 ¼-3 ¼ inches in diameter)
2 cups green beans, fresh or frozen

1. Heat the water in a large nonstick skillet over medium-high heat. Add the chopped onion and cook until translucent, stirring frequently, about 3 minutes.
2. Add apples, stirring often, until the apples are lightly golden, about 5 minutes.
3. Increase the heat to high, add the Chardonnay and allow the liquid to evaporate. Add the broth and herbs and stir. Reduce the heat and simmer for 5 minutes to reduce and thicken slightly.
4. Prick each potato with a fork several times and microwave on high 5 to 8 minutes. Remove the potatoes and wrap tightly in foil until serving.
5. Add the sausage to the onion and apple mixture; bring to a boil. Cover, reduce the heat, and simmer for 5 to 6 minutes, until sausages are warmed.
6. While the sausages are simmering, steam the green beans. To serve, divide the sausage and sauce, potatoes and green beans onto 4 plates.

Per serving *without mashed potatoes and green beans: 188 calories, 6 g fat, 65 g cholesterol, 525 mg sodium, 16 g carbohydrate, 0.75 g fiber, 17 g protein*

Per serving *with baked potatoes and green beans: 382 calories, 6 g fat, 65 mg cholesterol, 548 mg sodium, 60 g carbohydrate, 8.25 g fiber, 23 g protein*

Options:
- Substitute chopped or sliced chicken breasts for sausage.
- Substitute 1 cup TJ's Chunky Applesauce (without cinnamon) for the apples.

 Gluten-free

Chicken Taco Salad with Cilantro Dressing

If you have not tried Trader Joe's refrigerated Cilantro Salad Dressing, you are in for a treat. The creamy blend of citrus, spices, cilantro and cheese adds great flavor to salads and has many other uses as well. You can add it to yogurt as a topping for a burrito or tostada, or use it as a dip for vegetables. As you can see from the number of options below, this is a basic recipe and can be modified numerous ways.

Serves 4

2 cups (8 ounces) TJ's Just Chicken; frozen TJ's Just Grilled Chicken Strips, thawed; or 2 cups cooked chicken breast

1 cup black beans, drained and rinsed

1 cup frozen corn, thawed

¼ cup chopped red onion

2 cups TJ's Shredded Green Cabbage

½ avocado, sliced

¼ cup refrigerated TJ's Cilantro Salad Dressing

1 teaspoon fresh lime juice, optional

¼ cup chopped cilantro, optional

Per serving: 240 calories, 6.7 g fat, 43.2 mg cholesterol, 235 mg sodium, 25 g carbohydrate, 6.5 g fiber, 28 g protein

Options:
- Substitute shrimp for chicken.
- Substitute frozen TJ's Fire Roasted Corn for corn.
- Add TJ's Corn and Chile Tomato-Less Salsa.
- Substitute TJ's Corn and Chile Tomato-Less Salsa and TJ's Low Fat Parmesan Ranch dressing for the cilantro dressing.
- Place the taco salad in a tortilla and serve as a wrap.

Serve with:

Quick: TJ's Cornbread (290 calories and 12.5 g fat if you follow directions on the box and use the oil). If made with unsweetened applesauce in place of oil, it is only 190 calories/serving and 0.5 g fat. Save 100 calories and 12 grams of fat by making this substitution. You can use applesauce in place of the oil when you make it from scratch as well.

Super-quick: TJ's Organic Low Sodium Tomato and Roasted Red Pepper Soup (100 calories/cup)

Spicy Thai Noodle Bowls

This salad is crunchy and light, with just the right blend of Asian flavors. Purchase fresh ginger at Trader Joe's or buy minced ginger in a jar or tube in the produce section of a grocery store for convenience.

Serves 4

8 ounces thin rice noodles

2 cups (8 ounces) TJ's Just Chicken; frozen TJ's Just Grilled Chicken Strips, thawed; or 2 cups cooked chicken breast

½ (16 ounce) package TJ's Medium Cooked Shrimp, Tail Off, thawed and rinsed

3 cups shredded cabbage, preferably Napa cabbage

1 cup TJ's Shredded Carrots

1 red pepper, chopped

½ cup sliced red onion

1 English cucumber, cut in half lengthwise and then sliced on a bias

¾ cup TJ's Sesame Soy Ginger Vinaigrette

1 teaspoon fresh minced ginger or 2/3 teaspoon bottled minced ginger

⅓ teaspoon TJ's Crushed Garlic or 1 clove garlic, minced

¼ cup chopped roasted peanuts, for garnish

4 scallions, chopped, for garnish

¼ cup chopped cilantro, optional

1. Prepare noodles according to package directions; cool.

2. Combine the chicken, shrimp, cabbage, carrots, red pepper and cucumber in a large bowl.

3. Pour the salad dressing into a cup measure with a spout. Add the ginger and garlic and mix well. Pour over salad and toss until the salad is well coated.

4. Divide the noodles between four bowls. Top the noodles with the salad. Top the salad with chopped peanuts, sliced green onions and cilantro, if desired.

Per serving: 454 calories, 4.8 g fat, 30.5 mg cholesterol, 615 mg sodium, 53 g carbohydrate, 7.4 g fiber, 36 g protein

Options:

- Substitute Asian Style Spicy Peanut Vinaigrette for the Sesame Soy Ginger Vinaigrette.
- Add a few drops of Sweet Chili Sauce.
- Substitute 3 cups fresh TJ's Stir Fry Vegetables, including Napa cabbage, broccoli and snap peas, in place of shredded cabbage.
- Substitute TJ's Organic Baked Tofu, Teriyaki flavor, in place of chicken and shrimp.
- Substitute angel hair pasta for rice noodles.
- Substitute rice in place of noodles.

 Dairy-free

Serve with:

Quick: Broccoli with Lemon Zest (38 calories), page 165

Super quick: Steamed or microwaved broccoli florets

Basil Chicken Pasta

Here's a dish that's rich, creamy and low-fat. Can that be true? It can and is. Try it and see for yourself. Use fresh basil if you can for this dish, as fresh herbs (in this case, basil) add such wonderful flavor and aroma. You can freeze leftover basil in water in an ice cube tray and use it in soups and stews. It is adapted from a recipe by Diane Rattray, About.com Guide.

Serves 4

1 ½ cups (6 ounces) TJ's Organic Whole Wheat Rotelle Pasta (spiral pasta)
2 cups TJ's Broccoli Florets
1 cup TJ's Low Fat Sour Cream
2 teaspoons all-purpose flour
½ cup skim milk
1 ½ cups diced TJ's Just Grilled Chicken Strips or 1 ½ cups cooked chicken breast
¼ cup chopped basil or 1 teaspoon dried basil leaves
1 cup sliced mushrooms
4 tablespoons grated Parmesan cheese
¼ teaspoon salt, optional

1. Cook rotelle according to package directions. Add broccoli during the last 5 minutes of cooking time.
2. Meanwhile, in a large saucepan, combine sour cream and flour and blend well. Add milk and stir well. Cook over medium heat, stirring constantly, until thickened but not boiling.
3. Add chicken, basil, mushrooms and 3 tablespoons of the cheese. Stir frequently until thoroughly heated, about 4 minutes.
4. Drain rotelle and broccoli and add them to the large saucepan. Add the chicken and sauce and toss to coat. Sprinkle with remaining 1 tablespoon cheese when serving. Taste and add salt, if desired.

Per serving: 362 calories, 7.6 g fat, 52 mg cholesterol, 277 mg sodium, 38 g carbohydrate, 5 g fiber, 26 g protein

Serve with:
Quick: Amazing Watermelon Greek Salad with Feta Cheese (157 calories), page 84
Super-quick: Green salad with TJ's Fat Free Balsamic Vinaigrette

Honey Dijon Brown Rice with Chicken

This sweet and tangy chicken dish uses uncooked chicken that cooks quickly, as the chicken breasts are cut into bite-size pieces. You can also use a honey mustard blend instead of two separate products. Adapted from a recipe on Sparkpeople.com by Krylstalblu22.

Serves 4

2 pouches frozen TJ's Brown Rice
　　or 4 cups cooked brown rice
TJ's Extra Virgin Olive Oil Spray
16 ounces skinless, boneless
　　chicken breasts cut into
　　bite-size pieces
1 medium onion, chopped, or
　　1 cup TJ's Diced Onions
3 cups TJ's Broccoli Florets
2 cups crimini mushrooms, sliced
⅓ teaspoon TJ's Crushed Garlic or
　　1 clove, minced
6 tablespoons Dijon Mustard
2 tablespoons honey
2 tablespoons balsamic vinegar

1. Heat rice according to package instructions.
2. Spray a large skillet with cooking spray and heat over medium-high heat. Add cubed chicken. Cook chicken 3 to 5 minutes, until the chicken is brown and partially cooked.
3. Add onions and cook about 3 minutes, until onions become translucent. Add broccoli, mushrooms and garlic. Cook 4 to 5 minutes longer until veggies are tender yet crisp.
4. Combine mustard, honey and vinegar in a small bowl and stir into the chicken. Add the rice and stir well to combine. Cook for 2 to 3 minutes more.

Per serving: *369 calories, 1.4 g fat, 65 mg cholesterol, 564 mg sodium, 49 g carbohydrate, 4 g fiber, 32 g protein*

Option:
To lower sodium, use only 4 tablespoons of mustard and save 158 mg per serving.

Dairy-free

🚫 *Gluten-free if you use Trader Joe's mustard

Serve with:
Quick and Super-quick: Spinach salad with TJ's Fat Free Balsamic Vinaigrette

Ranch "Fried" Chicken

This has been one of my sons' favorites for years. It's so easy to make. While it's baking, you can make the side dishes. Use the ones suggested below, choose from other recipes in this cookbook or use TJ's frozen ready-to-use sides from the list on pages 174 to 175.

Serves 4

TJ's Extra Virgin Olive Oil Spray
½ cup TJ's Low Fat Parmesan
   Ranch Dressing
4 (4 ounce) boneless, skinless
   chicken breast halves
1 cup TJ's Garlic Mashed Potatoes
   flakes

1. Preheat oven to 450ºF. Coat a baking sheet with cooking spray.
2. Pour the dressing into a small bowl and place the potato flakes on a dinner plate.
3. Brush the dressing onto both sides of the chicken breasts. Roll the chicken breasts in the potato flakes.
4. Arrange chicken breasts on the baking pan, and place in the oven.
5. Turn the oven down to 350ºF and bake for 20 to 25 minutes, or until a meat thermometer placed into a chicken breast reads 170ºF.

Per serving: *207 calories, 4 g fat, 65 mg cholesterol, 436 mg sodium, 17 g carbohydrate, 0.7 g fiber, 23 g protein*

Option:
Use crushed corn flakes in place of instant mashed potatoes.

Serve with:
Quick: Hummus Soup (200 calories/serving), page 99, Lemon Asparagus with Parsley (45 calories/serving), page 164, and TJ's Roasted Potatoes with Peppers and Onions (70 calories/serving), page 20
Super-quick: Quinoa Duo with Vegetable Mélange (220 calories) and TJ's Beans so Green (90 calories/serving)

BBQ Chicken over Polenta

Could preparing dinner be this easy? Just add a vegetable (see suggestions below) and you're done. This dish is a little high in sodium, so make sure that your food choices throughout the day are lower in sodium.

Serves 4

4 tablespoons water or
  chicken broth
1 tube TJ's Organic Polenta
1 package refrigerated TJ's Pulled
  Chicken Breast in BBQ Sauce

1. In a large bowl, add water and polenta and mash polenta with a fork or potato masher until polenta is smooth.
2. Place polenta on a serving plate. Top with the chicken and sauce.
3. Cover and microwave 3 to 4 minutes, rotating after 1 ½ minutes, or bake at 350ºF for 20 minutes.

Per serving: *192 calories, 0.75 g fat, 38 mg cholesterol, 898 mg sodium, 13 g carbohydrate, 2 g fiber, 16 g protein*

Options:
- Add a sprinkling of Parmesan cheese.
- To reduce sodium, prepare your own polenta with little or no salt.

Serve with:
Quick: Quick Carrot and Beet Salad with Arugula (46 calories), page 77 and steamed broccoli
Super-quick: green salad with TJ's Fat Free Balsamic Vinaigrette and steamed broccoli

Chapter 11:

Seafood Entrées

Did you know that the American Heart Association recommends we eat seafood rich in omega-3 fatty acids at least twice a week to benefit our health? Even so, many people aren't sure which seafoods are the healthiest, and don't know how to prepare them in a healthy manner. If you're in this category, you are in luck, as there are many delicious, easy seafood recipes in this section.

Fish and seafood are low in saturated fat. They are a rich source of protein and iron, contain B-12 vitamins and have several health benefits. Fish is the richest source of omega-3 fatty acids, which may be helpful in the prevention and treatment of heart disease, high blood pressure, inflammation, mental health disorders, mood swings, depression, diabetes, digestive disorders, autoimmune disease and cancer. Our body doesn't make these fatty acids, so we have to get them from fish and other sources. Fish with the highest level of omega-3 fatty acids are those that live in cold water and include European anchovy, wild salmon, Pacific sardine, and rainbow trout. Moderate sources include albacore tuna canned in water, mussels, Alaskan King crab, shrimp and yellow fin tuna.

To stay abreast of which seafood is the best to eat, and which to avoid due to contaminants and other issues, go online to www.montereybayaquarium.org and then to SeafoodWatch.

Weight Watcher Points™ are available online at my website: www.HealthyTraderJoes.com.

Shrimp and Pineapple Curry

A wonderful combination of some of my favorite flavors: ginger, curry and coconut milk, with shrimp, sweet pineapple and a touch of lime. Add a little red curry paste if you want a little kick.

Serves 6

1 tablespoon water

1 clove garlic

⅓ teaspoon fresh minced ginger
   or bottled minced ginger

1 onion, chopped, or 1 cup
   TJ's Diced Onions

1 (16 ounce) package frozen
   TJ's Medium Shrimp, Tail Off,
   thawed and rinsed

2 cups TJ's Curry Simmer Sauce

1 cup TJ's Light Coconut Milk

1 cup frozen TJ's Pineapple Tidbits

⅛ to ¼ teaspoon red curry
   paste, optional

1 tablespoon lime juice

2 pouches frozen TJ's Brown Rice,
   or 4 cups cooked brown rice

Chopped cilantro, optional

1. Heat water in a large nonstick skillet over medium-high heat and cook onions until translucent, stirring frequently, about 3 minutes. Add garlic and ginger and stir about 1 minute more.
2. Add shrimp and stir for about 1 minute; add Curry Simmer Sauce, coconut milk and pineapple. Stir until heated through.
3. Heat rice according to package directions.
4. Add lime to the shrimp mixture; stir and serve over rice. Top with cilantro, optional.

Per serving: 292 calories, 6.6 g fat, 96 mg cholesterol, 752 mg sodium, 59 g carbohydrate, 5.9 g fiber, 21 g protein

Options:
- For more curry flavor, add 1 teaspoon curry powder.
- Add 1 cup cauliflower, broccoli, and/or pea pods.
- Use vermicelli in place of rice.
- Use basil in place of cilantro.

 Dairy-free

 *Gluten-free if you use Red Curry Paste from Thai Kitchen

Serve with:
Quick: Cauliflower with Curry Sauce (50 calories), page 166
Super-Quick: Cooked frozen or fresh peas or spinach

Venetian Seafood Medley

This gourmet seafood meal is perfect for a special occasion. If you don't have to watch your sodium closely, regular canned tomatoes or Trader Joe's regular chicken broth will work. If you don't have a zester for the lemon rind, you might want to get one the next time you are in one of those fun kitchen stores. They are very handy and zest from lemons, limes, oranges and citron adds so much flavor to lower-fat meals.

Serves 4

TJ's Extra Virgin Olive Oil Spray
1 tablespoon butter or margarine
1 (16 ounce) package frozen TJ's
   Seafood Blend
⅔ teaspoon TJ's Crushed Garlic or
   2 cloves garlic, minced
1 large shallot, finely chopped, or
   ½ cup chopped onion
½ teaspoon crushed red pepper
   flakes
⅔ cup dry white wine
⅔ cup TJ's Organic Low Sodium
   Chicken Broth or Vegetable
   Broth
1 (14 ounce) can TJ's Diced & No
   Salt Added Tomatoes in juice, or
   1 ½ cups chopped fresh
   tomatoes
¼ teaspoon tumeric or saffron
   threads
2 pouches frozen TJ's Brown Rice
   or 4 cups cooked rice
12 leaves fresh basil, shredded
   or torn
Zest from 1 lemon

1. Preheat a large skillet sprayed with olive oil spray over medium-high heat. Add butter. Add seafood blend and cook until lightly brown, about 6 to 7 minutes. Remove seafood from the pan.
2. Add the garlic, shallots and crushed red pepper flakes. Reduce heat and cook for 2 minutes, stirring constantly.
3. Add wine to the pan and cook for 1 minute, then add broth, tomatoes and turmeric or saffron threads. When the sauce comes to a simmer, return the seafood to the pan and heat for another 5 to 6 minutes.
4. Heat rice according to package directions and place it on individual plates. Spoon seafood and sauce over the rice and top with fresh basil and lemon zest.

Per serving: *320 calories, 3.8 g fat,*
130 mg cholesterol, 374 mg sodium,
43 g carbohydrate, 4.5 g fiber, 21 g protein

Options:
- Substitute 1 pound large shrimp or a combination of shrimp and scallops in place of seafood blend.
- Serve with pasta, quinoa or other grains in place of rice.

Serve with:
Quick and Super-quick: Steamed fresh or frozen asparagus or broccoli sprinkled with fresh lemon

Garlic Shrimp with Peppers

This is a great shortcut meal to prepare at the end of a long day. The brown rice, peppers, onions, and shrimp have already been cooked for you. The fire roasted peppers and onions add lots of flavor, as does the garlic and the 21 Salute Seasoning. It's almost like having a personal chef…almost.

Serves 4

2 pouches frozen TJ's Brown Rice or 4 cups cooked brown rice
½ cup TJ's Chicken Broth
1 ½ teaspoons cornstarch
1 package frozen TJ's Fired Roasted Bell Peppers and Onions
1 ⅓ teaspoons TJ's Crushed Garlic or 4 cloves minced
12 ounces frozen TJ's Cooked Medium Shrimp, Tail Off, thawed and rinsed
1 tablespoon margarine or butter
1 ½ tablespoons dry sherry
1 teaspoon TJ's 21 Seasoning Salute, or more to taste
¼ teaspoon red pepper flakes, optional
2 tablespoons chopped fresh parsley

1. Heat rice according to package directions and keep warm.
2. Stir broth and cornstarch together in a small bowl.
3. In a large nonstick skillet over medium-high heat, heat water and cook pepper mixture and garlic for about 3 minutes, stirring occasionally. Remove from pan and keep warm.
4. Add shrimp and margarine to the skillet and stir-fry shrimp over medium-high heat for 2 to 3 minutes. Add sherry and 21 Seasoning Salute.
5. Add cornstarch and broth blend to the shrimp and stir until thick and bubbly. Add vegetables and stir for 1 more minute, until coated with sauce.
6. Stir parsley into the rice. Serve shrimp over rice.

Per serving: 290 calories, 4.8 g fat, 117 g cholesterol, 306 mg sodium, 43.6 g carbohydrate, 4.5 g fiber, 28.5 g protein

Options:
- Add lemon.
- Substitute chicken or tofu in place of shrimp.
- Substitute ¾ pound linguine in place of rice.

 *Dairy-free if you use margarine and not butter

 *Gluten-free if use TJ's Organic Free Range or Organic Low Sodium Broth

Serve with:
Quick and super quick: Spinach salad with TJ's Fat Free Balsamic Vinaigrette

Honey Mustard Salmon

I've been preparing this simple, sweet and tangy recipe for years. It is a great dish to serve to guests, as it can cook while you and your guests socialize or enjoy a first course.

Serves 4

4 salmon fillets, 5 to 6 ounces each
1 ½ tablespoons honey
1 ½ tablespoons TJ's Dijon
    mustard
1-2 tablespoons fresh lime juice
¼ cup cornmeal
½ teaspoon dried thyme
TJ's Extra Virgin Olive Oil Spray

1. Preheat oven to 375ºF.
2. Rinse fillets and pat dry.
3. Whisk together honey, mustard and lime juice in a shallow bowl. Combine cornmeal and thyme in a separate bowl.
4. Place salmon on a baking pan sprayed with olive oil spray.
5. Spoon honey sauce over the salmon fillets. Sprinkle the herbed cornmeal on top and bake, uncovered, for 20 to 30 minutes or until salmon flakes easily with a fork.

Per serving: 314 calories, 11.5 g fat, 100 mg cholesterol, 200 mg sodium, 12 g carbohydrate, 0.5 g fiber, 36.6 g protein

 Dairy-free

 Gluten-free

Serve with:
Quick: Broccoli Salad with Grapes and Raisins (160 calories), page 83
Super-quick: Country Potatoes with Haricot Verts and Wild Mushrooms (130 calories), and steamed frozen or fresh broccoli

Halibut with Herb Sauce

I first served this at a summer dinner party and my friend, Kathleen, who often dines at fine restaurants, raved about it. It's so simple, too.

Serves 6

6 tablespoons fresh lemon juice
3 tablespoons extra virgin olive oil
3 tablespoons chopped fresh basil
3 tablespoons chopped chives
3 tablespoons chopped fresh
  parsley
TJ's Extra Virgin Olive Oil Spray
6 (6 ounce) halibut fillets
¼ teaspoon sea salt
¼ teaspoon freshly ground pepper

1. Purée lemon juice, 2 tablespoons and 1 teaspoon of the olive oil, basil, chives and parsley in a small food processor or blender.
2. Preheat broiler. Wash the fish and pat dry with a paper towel. Lightly brush the fish with the remaining two teaspoons olive oil and sprinkle with sea salt and pepper.
3. Spray a baking pan with olive oil spray and place the halibut fillets on the sheet. Broil halibut until just opaque in the center, about 5 minutes per side.
4. Transfer fish to dinner plates and spoon sauce over each fillet before serving.

Per serving: *301 calories, 11 g fat, 69 mg cholesterol, 214 mg sodium, 1.3 g carbohydrate, 0 g fiber, 45 g protein*

Option:
Substitute cod, flounder, tilapia or other white fish for halibut.

 Dairy-free

 Gluten-free

Serve with:
Quick: Carrot and Beet Salad with Arugula (46 calories), page 77, Kale and Quinoa Pilaf (218 calories), page 169 and steamed green beans with lemon or other seasoning
Super-quick: Penne Arrabliata or Penne Pepperonete (200 calories/serving each) and frozen TJ's Asparagus Spears with seasoning of your choice

Glazed Apricot Salmon

It doesn't get any easier than this! And wait until you taste this fabulous dish. This recipe is adapted from one by Sam Zien, The Cooking Guy.

Note: The nutritional analysis is a bit misleading. The sauce spreads, and unless you scoop it up and put it over the rice, about 1/3 of it is left on the pan.

Serves 6

1 cup TJ's Reduced Sugar Apricot
   Preserves
⅓ cup TJ's General Tsao Sauce or
   Black Bean and Garlic Sauce
TJ's Extra Virgin Olive Oil Spray
2 pounds wild Silverbrite or other
   salmon fillet
2 tablespoons green onions, finely
   chopped
Sesame seeds, optional

1. Preheat the broiler to high. Cover a cookie sheet or pizza pan with foil to make clean up easier.
2. Combine apricot preserves and General Tsao sauce in a small bowl and mix well.
3. Lay the salmon on the foil-covered baking sheet. Spoon the sauce over the top of the salmon and broil for 7 minutes for each inch of salmon thickness.
4. Remove the salmon to a platter and sprinkle with the green onions and sesame seeds, if desired.

Per serving: 385 calories, 12 g fat, 107 mg cholesterol, 259 mg sodium, 29 g carbohydrate, 0 g fiber, 39 g protein

 Dairy-free

Serve with:
Quick: Spinach Salad with Peanut Vinaigrette (102 calories), page 80 and Broccoli with Lemon Zest (38 calories), page 165
Super quick: Green salad with TJ's Champagne Pear Vinaigrette and TJ's Quinoa with Vegetable Mélange (220 calories)

Spicy Orange Shrimp

Here's an easy, sweet yet spicy shrimp dish that uses seasonings you probably have in your cupboard. This recipe is adapted from one in *The Express Lane* cookbook.

Serves 4

1 teaspoon water

⅔ teaspoon TJ's Crushed Garlic or 2 cloves, minced

2 cups TJ's Broccoli Florets

1 pound TJ's Cooked Medium Shrimp, Tail Off, thawed and rinsed

1 ½ cups orange juice

1-2 teaspoons Tabasco or other hot sauce

2 teaspoons Worcestershire Sauce

2 teaspoons light brown sugar

¼ teaspoon salt

1 tablespoon cornstarch stirred into 1 tablespoon water

2 pouches frozen TJ's Brown Rice or 4 cups cooked brown rice

1. In a large nonstick skillet, heat water and add garlic; cook for 1 minute.

2. Add broccoli and stir frequently until broccoli is crisp-tender, about 2 minutes.

3. Stir in orange juice, Tabasco sauce, Worcestershire sauce, brown sugar and salt. Bring to a boil and boil for 2 minutes. Add shrimp and stir frequently until shrimp is warm, about 3 minutes.

4. Dissolve cornstarch in the water and continue cooking, stirring until the sauce thickens, 2 to 3 minutes.

5. Heat rice in the microwave. Serve shrimp and broccoli over rice.

Per serving: 341 calories, 2.25 g fat, 146 mg cholesterol, 600 mg sodium, 50.7 g carbohydrate, 3.2 g fiber, 27.25 g protein

Options:

- Substitute snow peas or Brussels sprouts for the broccoli.
- Add chopped green onions.
- Substitute chicken or tofu for the shrimp.
- Substitute TJ's Seafood Medley for the shrimp.

 Dairy-free

 *Gluten-free if you use a gluten-free Worcestershire sauce (Lea and Perrins® (made in the U.S.) and French's® brands are both gluten-free)

Serve with:

Quick: Hearts of Palm Salad (30 calories), page 79
Super-quick: Green salad with TJ's Low Fat Parmesan Ranch Dressing

Ahi Tuna and Vegetables with Sesame Soy Ginger Sauce

Prepackaged stir-fry meals can contain a lot of sodium. By using the ingredients in this recipe, you can have the convenience without the extra sodium.

To thaw tuna: place in the refrigerator for 24 hours per pound of fish, put the fish under cold running water until it is flexible, or microwave on the lowest defrost setting until it is defrosted. Didn't get around to thawing it? Just stir-fry the fish slices a couple of minutes longer or until seared. Trader Joe's fish is frozen just after it's caught, unlike other frozen fish that may be frozen twice, and has no preservatives.

Serves 4

6 ounces dry TJ's Asian Rice Sticks or linguine

1 teaspoon TJ's Toasted Sesame Oil

12 ounces (¾ pound) frozen TJ's Ahi Tuna Steaks, thawed or partially thawed

⅓ teaspoon TJ's Crushed Garlic, or 1 clove, minced

1 teaspoon minced fresh ginger or ½ teaspoon bottled minced ginger

1 package frozen TJ's Stir Fry Vegetables or refrigerated Asian Stir Fry

½ cup frozen TJ's Pineapple Tidbits, or fresh or canned pineapple

½ cup TJ's Sesame Soy Ginger Vinaigrette

¼ cup sliced green onions

1. Cook noodles according to package directions and keep warm.
2. Cut tuna into ¼-inch slices. Heat oil in a large nonstick skillet over medium-high heat. Add tuna and stir-fry 3 to 4 minutes, or until tuna is seared. Remove from heat and keep warm.
3. Add garlic, ginger, vegetables and pineapple to skillet and stir-fry until vegetables are cooked, about 6 minutes. Add vinaigrette and tuna and stir about 2 minutes longer or until heated.
4. Divide noodles between four plates and top with tuna and vegetables. Garnish with green onions.

Per serving: *326 calories, 2.6 g fat, 45 mg cholesterol, 277 mg sodium, 56 g carbohydrate, 3 g fiber, 22.5 g protein*

Option:
Substitute salmon or shark for ahi tuna.

 Dairy-free

Serve with:
Quick: Ginger Garlic Broccoli, (60 calories), page 168
Super Quick: frozen TJ's Grilled Asparagus Spears with a dab of sesame oil

Tilapia Tapenade

Want dinner quickly? This dish couldn't be easier or tastier. If the tilapia isn't completely thawed, bake it 5 minutes longer and check to make sure it is cooked before serving.

Serves 4

TJ's Extra Virgin Olive Oil Spray
4 (4 ounce) tilapia fillets, thawed
8 tablespoons TJ's Roasted Red
    Pepper and Artichoke Tapenade

1. Preheat the oven to 375ºF. Spray a 9 x 13-inch baking dish with olive oil cooking spray.
2. Place the fillets in the baking dish and top each with 2 tablespoons of tapenade.
3. Cover the dish with foil and bake for 25 to 30 minutes. Fish is done when it flakes easily with a fork.

Per serving: 154 calories, 2.8 g fat, 45 mg cholesterol, 85.5 mg sodium, 4 g carbohydrate, 1 g fiber, 22.75 g protein

Options:

- Substitute TJ's Olive Tapenade Spread or others in place of Roasted Red Pepper and Artichoke Tapenade.
- Poach fish in a little water in a nonstick skillet for 6 minutes. Drain water and top fish with tapenade. Cover and turn heat to medium; cook until tapenade is warm, about 4 minutes.
- Add your favorite frozen vegetables to the pan and cook along with the fish.

 Dairy-free

 Gluten-free

Serve with:

Quick: Hummus Soup (200 calories), page 99, Orzo Spinach Salad (114 calories), page 82
Super-Quick: frozen TJ's Quinoa Duo with Vegetable Mélange (220 calories), and frozen green beans

Broiled Shrimp with Papaya Mango Salsa

Use raw shrimp in this recipe for a crispy result. Using Trader Joe's Papaya Mango Salsa makes this recipe a snap to prepare and adds a sweet yet tart flavor to the shrimp.

Serves 4

1 pound TJ's Uncooked Jumbo Shrimp, peeled and deveined, tails off, rinsed and patted dry

1 teaspoon chili powder

¾ teaspoon ground cumin

½ teaspoon paprika

¼ teaspoon freshly ground black pepper

1 teaspoon extra virgin olive oil

2 tablespoons water

1 (12 ounce) package fresh TJ's Spinach

2 pouches frozen TJ's Brown Rice or 4 cups cooked brown rice

½ container fresh TJ's Papaya Mango Salsa

1 teaspoon fresh lime juice, optional

¼ cup fresh chopped cilantro, optional

1. In a medium bowl, combine shrimp, chili powder, ground cumin, paprika, black pepper and olive oil. Toss to coat.
2. Put water in a large skillet and add the spinach. Turn the heat to high and shake the pan until the spinach has wilted. Drain and keep warm.
3. Preheat the broiler. Coat a broiler pan with cooking spray. Place shrimp on the broiler pan in a single layer. Broil 4 to 6 inches from the heat for 5 minutes, or until the shrimp is opaque.
4. While shrimp are cooking, heat rice according to package directions.
5. Divide spinach on 4 plates. Top with the rice, shrimp and then salsa. Top with lime juice and cilantro, if desired.

Per serving: 352 calories, 4 g fat, 173 mg cholesterol, 607 mg sodium, 16 g carbohydrate, 4 g fiber, 29 g protein

Options:
- Add chopped frozen mango cubes to salsa before topping shrimp.
- Substitute TJ's Smoky, Spicy, Peach Salsa for Papaya Mango Salsa.
- Substitute other grains such as quinoa or TJ's frozen Rice Medley in place of rice.

*Dairy-free if you use TJ's Smoky, Spicy, Peach Salsa in place of TJ's Papaya Mango Salsa

*Gluten-free if you use TJ's Smoky, Spicy, Peach Salsa in place of TJ's Papaya Mango Salsa

Serve with:
Quick: Lemony Asparagus with Parsley (45 calories), page 164
Super-quick: TJ's Grilled Asparagus Spears (25 calories)

Wild Rice Crab Salad

As you may already know, wild rice isn't really rice but the seed of an aquatic grass that has twice the fiber and protein of brown rice. It gives a nutty texture to this wonderful salad. You can make twice as much and freeze the leftover rice for the next time you want to use cooked wild rice in this or other dishes. You can make the dressing ahead of time and chill it.

Serves 6

1 cup TJ's Wild Rice, uncooked
   (3 cups cooked)
½ cup thinly sliced green onion
1 large tomato, peeled, seeded
   and diced
8 ounces fresh cooked crab meat,
   or 1 (7 ounce) can crab meat,
   rinsed and drained
1 cup thinly sliced celery or fennel
Salt and pepper, optional

Dressing:

⅓ cup TJ's Reduced Fat
   Mayonnaise
⅓ cup TJ's Low Fat Sour Cream
¼ cup TJ's Chili Pepper Sauce
1 tablespoon lemon juice
1 teaspoon Dijon mustard

1. Cook wild rice according to package directions.
2. Combine wild rice, green onion, tomato, seafood and celery in a large bowl.
3. Combine dressing ingredients in a medium bowl and whisk. Add to wild rice mixture and toss well. Taste and add salt and pepper, if desired. Chill for at least 30 minutes to allow flavors to develop.

Per serving: 209 calories, 11.6 g fat, 6.5 mg cholesterol, 260 mg sodium, 38.7 g carbohydrate, 2.8 g fiber, 13 protein

Options:

- Substitute 1 (5 ounce) can tuna in water instead of crab.
- Substitute low- or nonfat yogurt in place of mayonnaise or sour cream.
- Substitute TJ's Non Fat Sour Cream for Low Fat Sour Cream.

*Dairy-free if you use soy yogurt or 2/3 cup reduced fat mayonnaise

Gluten-free

Serve with:
Quick and Super-quick:

TJ's Low Sodium Tomato and Roasted Red Pepper Soup with ¼ teaspoon cumin per serving and a dollop of plain low-fat yogurt (110 calories, 140 mg sodium/serving)

Shrimp Curry with Snow Peas

I thought I'd tried almost every combination of ingredients using Curry Simmer Sauce in my *Quick and Healthy Meals from Trader Joe's* cookbook and was very pleased to create at least one more dish with it. I will be making this often!

Serves 6

1 tablespoon water

1 large onion, thinly sliced

1 pound frozen TJ's Large Cooked Shrimp, Tail Off, thawed and rinsed

½ cup TJ's Curry Simmer Sauce

1 (5 ounce) package TJ's Snow Peas

3 medium tomatoes, chopped

2 pouches frozen TJ's Brown Rice or 4 cups cooked brown rice

½ (14 ounce) can TJ's Light Coconut Milk

2 tablespoons fresh lemon or lime juice

1 (6 ounce) package TJ's Baby Spinach, or 6 cups fresh spinach

¼ cup chopped fresh basil, Thai basil or cilantro

1. In a large nonstick skillet, heat water and cook onion over medium-high heat until translucent, about 3 minutes.
2. Add the shrimp and the Curry Simmer Sauce and stir to prevent sticking, for about 2 minutes. Add the snow peas and tomatoes and cook for 2 more minutes.
3. Heat rice according to package directions.
4. Add the coconut milk, lemon or lime juice and spinach to the shrimp and simmer until the spinach has wilted. Stir in the basil or cilantro. Serve hot over the rice.

Per serving: 248 calories, 4.5 g fat, 77 mg cholesterol, 576 mg sodium, 32 g carbohydrate, 5 g fiber, 20 g protein

Options:
- Substitute TJ's Thai Yellow (or Red) Curry Sauce for Curry Simmer Sauce, or use a combination of curry sauces.
- Add other vegetables such as broccoli, cauliflower, cabbage, etc.

 Dairy-free

 Gluten-free

Serve with:
Quick: Broccoli Peanut Slaw (90 calories), page 81
Super Quick: Make a salad with fresh TJ's Stir Fry Vegetables (Napa cabbage, broccoli and snow peas) and add TJ's Asian Style Spicy Peanut Vinaigrette

Teriyaki Salmon Cakes

These slightly sweet salmon cakes are terrific when topped with a little pickled ginger or wasabi. Most canned salmon, including TJ's, is wild and full of omega-3 fats, which help reduce inflammation, improve the body's ability to respond to insulin and help prevent cancer cell growth.

Serves 4

1 (14.75 ounce) can salmon, rinsed, drained, and flaked
2 teaspoons minced fresh ginger or bottled minced ginger
2 tablespoons chopped green onions
1 tablespoon lemon juice
1 tablespoon reduced sodium soy sauce, or tamari
1 tablespoon TJ's Soyaki or Teriyaki sauce
½ cup whole grain crackers (5 Ak-mak), crushed
2 large eggs, lightly beaten; or 4 egg whites
¼ cup chopped minced cilantro
TJ's Extra Virgin Olive Oil Spray
2 tablespoons pickled ginger or wasabi, optional

1. Preheat oven to 400°F.
2. In a medium bowl, combine the salmon, ginger, green onions, lemon juice, soy sauce and Soyaki sauce, using a rubber spatula. Stir in the crackers, eggs and cilantro; mix to combine.
3. Divide the salmon mixture into quarters and form into four 1-inch thick patties. Refrigerate for at least 30 minutes or overnight before cooking.
4. Spray a large, heavy skillet on medium-high heat with cooking spray. Add the salmon patties and cook until golden brown on one side, about 2 minutes. Flip and cook the other side for about 2 minutes. Transfer patties to a baking sheet and bake for 8 minutes, until golden.

Per serving: 240 calories, 12 g fat, 176 mg cholesterol, 754 mg sodium, 11 g carbohydrate, 1.8 g fiber, 12.5 g protein

Per serving with 4 egg whites replacing 2 eggs: 219 calories, 10 g fat, 70 mg cholesterol, 777 mg sodium, 11 g carbohydrate, 1.8 g fiber, 16.5 g protein

 *Dairy-free if used TJ's canned salmon

Serve with:
Quick: Refrigerated TJ's Stir Fry Vegetables stir-fried with a little sesame oil and soy sauce or tamari, and heated frozen TJ's Brown Rice (160 calories/cup)
Super-quick: Frozen TJ's Stir Fry Vegetables stir-fried in water with a bit of General Tsao sauce or Soyaki Sauce, served with heated TJ's Frozen Brown Rice (160 calories/cup)

Seared Chili-Flavored Tuna

This is my new favorite way to cook tuna. The chili powder adds just the right amount of punch and it couldn't be easier.

Did you know that most of the spices in kitchen cabinets only last about a year before they lose their flavor? It's a good idea to put a date on the spice containers when you first open them, so that you can replace them after a year and ensure that your food remains flavorful.

Serves 4

1 teaspoon chili powder
½ teaspoon pepper
¼ teaspoon salt
4 (4 ounce) Ahi Tuna Steaks or
   2 (8 ounce) steaks, about 1 inch
   thick, thawed if frozen
TJ's Extra Virgin Olive Oil Spray

1. In a small bowl, blend chili powder, pepper and salt.
2. Rinse the fish and pat dry with paper towels. Sprinkle the spices over both sides of the ahi.
3. Spray a large nonstick skillet over medium-high heat with the oil spray.
4. Add the fish and cook for about 4 minutes on each side, or until fish flakes easily with a fork. If you are cooking 2 larger steaks, cut them in half. Serve warm.

Per serving: 120 calories, 1.5 g fat, 60 mg cholesterol, 185 mg sodium, 4 g carbohydrate, 0 g fiber, 25 g protein

Options:
- Use 2 teaspoons grapeseed oil in place of olive oil spray for a fish that is a bit more moist.
- Top fish with TJ's Papaya Mango Salsa or TJ's Smoky, Spicy, Peach Salsa.
- Slice tuna and use as a filling for tacos.
- Top with TJ's Papaya Mango Salsa, chopped cabbage, and a squirt of fresh lime.
- Top with a mixture of TJ's Cilantro Salad Dressing and nonfat or low-fat yogurt.
- Top ahi with fresh salsa.

 Dairy-free

 Gluten-free

Serve with:
Quick: Amazing Watermelon Salad (157 calories), page 84, Brussels sprouts (53 calories), page 163 and Kale and Quinoa Pilaf (218 calories), page 169
Super-quick: Fresh spinach salad with TJ's Cilantro Salad Dressing, Fire Roasted Vegetables with Balsamic Butter Sauce (70 calories), and Quinoa Duo with Vegetable Mélange (220 calories)

Shrimp Jambalaya

A blend of seasonings spices up this traditionally high fat, high sodium dish. To reduce sodium even further, replace half of the shrimp (as they are much higher in sodium than chicken breast) with uncooked, diced chicken breast and cook a few minutes longer.

Serves 6

2 tablespoons chicken broth

3 stalks celery, chopped

1 medium onion, chopped or
   1 cup TJ's Diced Onions

1 cup frozen TJ's Mélange à Trois
   (mixed bell pepper)

3 ½ cups TJ's chicken broth

2 pouches frozen TJ's Brown Rice
   or 4 cups cooked brown rice

2 (15 ounce) cans TJ's Diced &
   No Salt Added Tomatoes,
   partially drained; or 3 cups
   coarsely chopped tomatoes
   (about 3 large)

¼ cup chopped fresh parsley

½ teaspoon dried thyme leaves

¼ teaspoon garlic powder

¼ teaspoon salt

¼ teaspoon pepper

¼-½ teaspoon cayenne, or more
   to taste

1 (16 ounce) package TJ's Cooked
   Medium Shrimp, Tail Off

¼ cup chopped parsley

1. Heat broth in a large nonstick saucepan over medium-high heat. Add celery, onion and peppers. Cook 5 minutes, stirring occasionally.

2. Stir in all remaining ingredients except shrimp. Bring to a boil. Reduce heat and simmer 8 minutes.

3. Add shrimp and cook until shrimp are thoroughly heated, about 3 minutes. To serve, spoon into 6 individual bowls. Garnish with chopped parsley. Serve with crusty French bread.

Per serving: 297 calories, 1.7 g fat, 97 mg cholesterol, 486 mg sodium, 29 g carbohydrate, 4 g fiber, 18.6 g protein

Options:

- Substitute cubed chicken in place of shrimp or use half shrimp and half chicken.
- Add smoked turkey sausage, skin removed.

 Dairy-free

 * Gluten-free if use TJ's Organic Free Range Chicken Broth or Organic Low Sodium Chicken Broth

Serve with:

Quick: Green salad with TJ's Cilantro Salad Dressing and TJ's Cornbread (290 calories and 12.5 g fat if you follow directions on the box and use the oil). If made with unsweetened applesauce in place of oil, it is only 190 calories/serving and 0.5 g fat. Save 100 calories and 12 grams of fat by making this substitution. You can use applesauce in place of the oil when you make it from scratch as well.

Super-quick:
Green salad with Cilantro Salad Dressing

Chapter 12:

Vegetarian Entrées

Whether you are a vegetarian, want to add some vegetarian meals to your menus or are cooking for a vegetarian, you will find these meals easy and flavorful. Many of the recipes are also vegan (contain no animal products).

Weight Watcher Points™ are available online at my website: www.HealthyTraderJoes.com.

Cuban Black Beans with Fried Rice

This flavorful vegetarian dish combines beans, pineapple, peppers, spices and rice, and takes minutes to prepare.

Serves 3

2 teaspoons water

⅔ teaspoon TJ's Crushed Garlic or 2 cloves garlic, minced

½ onion, chopped or ½ cup TJ's Diced Onions

¾ cup TJ's Cuban Black Beans

1 cup frozen TJ's Pineapple Tidbits, TJ's Canned Pineapple, drained, or fresh pineapple, diced

2 cups frozen TJ's Fire Roasted Bell Peppers and Onions

2 teaspoons ground cumin

¼ teaspoon cayenne pepper

2 cups frozen TJ's Brown Rice, or 4 cups cooked brown rice

1 teaspoon lime juice

¼ cup chopped cilantro

2 tablespoons TJ's Cilantro Salad Dressing

1. In a large nonstick skillet over medium-high heat, add water and cook garlic and onion until onion becomes translucent, about 3 minutes.
2. Add black beans, pineapple, mixed peppers and rice and cook, stirring continually until rice is heated and lightly brown.
3. Add lime, cilantro and salad dressing and stir gently until blended.

Per serving: 196 calories, 0 g fat, 0 mg cholesterol, 168 mg sodium, 36 g carbohydrate, 6.7 g fiber, 7.7 g protein

Options:

- Use the filling for a burrito.
- Add chicken or shrimp for a non-vegetarian entrée with more protein.
- Sprinkle lower-fat Monterey Jack or part skim mozzarella cheese over the finished dish and let it melt before serving.

Serve with:

Quick: 4 ears corn on the cob (140 calories/ear)

Super-quick: Roasted Red Pepper and Lentil Soup (230 calories/serving), page 101

Hummus Pizza

These pizzas are quick to make and are very tasty. Vary the type of hummus to suit your taste.

Serves 4

4 TJ's Whole Wheat Middle Eastern
   Flatbreads
1 (7 ounce) container TJ's Tomato
   and Basil Hummus
½ (7.4 ounce) jar TJ's Fire Roasted
   Red Peppers, sliced thinly
   (about 1 cup sliced)
2 green onions, chopped
½ English cucumber, sliced thinly
½ cup TJ's Black Olives, sliced
2 tablespoons TJ's Crumbled Fat
   Free Feta Cheese
2 tablespoons chopped parsley,
   optional
Sliced red onions, optional

1. Preheat oven to 400ºF.
2. Evenly spread hummus over
   4 flatbreads and top with red
   peppers, cucumber, green
   onions and black olives. Add feta
   cheese and optional ingredients,
   if desired.
3. Bake 400ºF for 10 to 12 minutes
   or until edges of flatbread
   become slightly brown. Serve
   warm or at room temperature.

Per serving: *254 calories, 8 g fat, 0.75 mg cholesterol, 702 mg sodium, 38 g carbohydrate, 6.6 g fiber, 8.8 g protein*

Options:
- Add artichoke hearts.
- To reduce sodium, use fresh red peppers, lower-sodium hummus or omit olives.
- Substitute TJ's Naan, tortillas or bread in place of flatbreads.

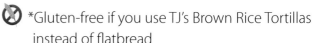 *Gluten-free if you use TJ's Brown Rice Tortillas instead of flatbread

Serve with:
Quick: Lemony Asparagus with Parsley (45 calories), page 164
Super-quick: Assorted raw vegetables and TJ's Tzatzki as a dip

Peanut Curry Tofu

I often put a few ingredients together to see what they will taste like. Usually the concoctions taste pretty good but this one was fantastic, if I do say so myself.

Serves 4

1 cup TJ's Curry Simmer Sauce
1 cup (5 ounces) TJ's Firm Tofu, mashed with a fork
1 ⅓ tablespoons natural style peanut butter, creamy or chunky
1⅓ tablespoons TJ's Reduced Sugar Apricot Spread
2 pouches frozen TJ's Brown Rice or 4 cups cooked brown rice
2 green onions, sliced
¼ cup chopped cilantro, optional
¼ cup chopped peanuts, optional

1. Combine simmer sauce, tofu, peanut butter and apricot spread in a medium saucepan or microwave bowl. Heat over medium heat for 8 to10 minutes, stirring often, or microwave about 2 minutes until warm.
2. Heat rice according to package directions and keep warm.
3. Serve tofu over rice and add green onions. Add cilantro and peanuts, if desired.

Per serving: *234 calories, 6 g fat, 0 mg cholesterol, 404 mg sodium, 30.8 g carbohydrate, 4.2 g fiber, 11 g protein*

Option:
Substitute other Trader Joe's simmer sauces in place of Curry Simmer Sauce.

Ⓧ Gluten-free

V Vegan

Serve with:
Quick: Broccoli Peanut Slaw (90 calories), page 81
Super-quick: TJ's Harvest Hodgepodge, steamed or microwaved, with TJ's Asian Style Spicy Peanut Vinaigrette

Grilled Eggplant Mélange and Cannellini Beans

My book group gave this dish two thumbs up when I asked them to taste it. My class participants were also very enthusiastic about it. The combination of the whole wheat pasta, frozen eggplant and zucchini and cannellini beans delivers a whopping 10 grams of fiber, and it is very easy to prepare.

Serves 4

8 ounces TJ's Whole Wheat Rotelle
1 package frozen TJ's Grilled
    Eggplant and Zucchini Mélange
½ (15.5 ounce) can cannellini
    beans, rinsed and drained
1 tablespoon fresh chopped basil
¼ cup Parmesan cheese, optional

1. Cook tortellini according to package directions, keep warm.
2. Add beans to mélange and heat according to package directions. Add chopped basil and mix well. Serve over pasta and top with Parmesan, if desired.

Per serving: 332 calories, 3 g fat, 6.6 mg cholesterol, 368 mg sodium, 58 g carbohydrate, 10 g fiber, 15 g protein

Options:
- Substitute ½ regular pasta and ½ whole wheat if you or others aren't yet used to eating 100% whole wheat pasta.
- Add chopped cooked chicken for a non-vegetarian version.

Serve with:

Quick: Steamed chopped zucchini, green beans and mushrooms topped with a little olive oil and basil, topped with TJ's Fat Free Balsamic Vinaigrette (about 60 calories per cup depending on how much olive oil is used)

Super-quick: TJ's Fire Roasted Vegetables with Balsamic Butter (70 calories)

Tortellini with Roasted Red Pepper Sauce

Roasted red pepper sauce takes just a few minutes to make. You'll have a gourmet dish in minutes.

Serves 4

1 (10 ounce) package fresh TJ's Cheese Tortellini

2 TJ's Fire Roasted Red Peppers from a 12 ounce jar

2 teaspoons vinegar from the roasted red pepper jar

TJ's Extra Virgin Olive Oil Spray

2 teaspoons water

1 teaspoon TJ's Crushed Garlic or 3 cloves garlic, minced

¼ cup red wine

Pinch of salt

Pinch of pepper

½ cup fresh grated Parmesan cheese

1 tablespoon skim milk

1-3 teaspoons fresh basil, chopped

1. Cook tortellini according to package directions; keep warm.
2. Place peppers and vinegar in a blender and purée.
3. Spray a medium nonstick skillet with the oil spray and place over medium-high heat. Add water and heat. Add garlic and sauté 30 seconds, stirring constantly.
4. Add pepper purée and sauté 1 to 2 minutes more.
5. Stir in red wine and cook for 1 to 2 minutes. Add salt and pepper.
6. Add cheese and milk and stir for 2 minutes to blend the sauce.
7. Add cooked tortellini and stir until warmed through. Sprinkle with basil and serve.

Per serving: 258 calories, 6 g fat, 37 mg cholesterol, 473 mg sodium, 32 g carbohydrate, 2 g fiber, 13.8 g protein

Serve with:
Quick: Green Salad with Figs and TJ's Champagne Pear Vinaigrette (122 calories), page 76
Super-quick: TJ's Cauliflower Romanesco Basilica (70 calories/serving)

Spicy Sweet Potato and Black Bean Burrito for One

While you can double or quadruple this recipe to make more burritos, sometimes it's nice to have a simple recipe for a meal for one, especially if you are putting it together from leftovers.

Serves 1

½ cup TJ's Refried Black Beans with Jalapeño Peppers
⅓ cup cooked sweet potato
1 tablespoon TJ's Spicy, Smoky, Peach Salsa
2 drops hot sauce or TJ's Sweet Chili Sauce
1 TJ's Whole Wheat Tortilla
Chopped cilantro, optional

1. Place all of the ingredients except cilantro in a saucepan on medium heat and heat for 4 to 5 minutes.
2. Heat the tortilla in the oven or microwave.
3. Place the filling inside the warmed tortilla, sprinkle with cilantro, if desired, and wrap.

Per serving: 282 calories, 1 g fat, 0 mg cholesterol, 662 mg sodium, 58.2 g carbohydrate, 12.7 g fiber, 13.3 g protein

Options:

- Use TJ's Cuban Black Beans in place of refried black beans.
- Add low-fat cheese.
- Add chopped tomatoes.
- Add slightly cooked chopped zucchini.
- Use filling as a dip for lower fat tortilla chips or vegetables.
- Top with nonfat or low-fat yogurt or a dab of TJ's Cilantro Salad Dressing.

 *Gluten-free if you use a TJ's Brown Rice Tortilla in place of a whole wheat tortilla.

Vegan

Serve with:

Quick: Steamed TJ's Soycutash topped with a little salsa (100 calories)

Super-quick: TJ's Low Sodium Tomato and Roasted Red Pepper Soup with ¼ teaspoon cumin per cup and chopped cilantro (100 calories per cup), and warmed corn or whole wheat tortilla

Indian Rice Curry

Here's another simple, flavorful meal made easier with precooked brown rice. Even though it is low in calories, fat and sodium, it is very filling. This recipe is adapted from one in the *Diabetic Meals in 30 Minutes-or Less!* cookbook.

Serves 4

2 teaspoons water
1 small onion, minced, or ½ cup
   TJ's Diced Onions
¼ cup chopped tart apple
2 teaspoons curry powder
Dash cayenne pepper
2 pouches frozen TJ's Brown Rice
   or 4 cups cooked brown rice
1 (15 ounce) can garbanzo beans,
   rinsed and drained
1 tablespoon fresh lemon juice
Fresh ground pepper

1. In a large nonstick skillet over medium heat, heat the water and sauté onions for about 3 minutes.
2. Add chopped apple and sauté 3 minutes more. Add curry powder and cayenne and stir so that apple and onions are coated.
3. Add cooked rice and garbanzo beans and stir. Heat until the rice and beans are warm, about 3 minutes. Sprinkle with lemon juice, add pepper and serve.

Per serving: 270 calories, 1.9 g fat, 0 mg cholesterol, 262 mg sodium, 52 g carbohydrate, 6.8 g fiber, 9.5 g protein

 Gluten-free

 Vegan

Serve with:
Quick: Cauliflower with Curry Sauce (50 calories), page 166
Super-quick: TJ's Low Sodium Butternut Squash Soup with 1 tablespoon TJ's Curry Simmer Sauce (113 calories per cup)

Indonesian Curried Tempeh

You may be new to tempeh, but it has been a staple in Indonesia for over 2,000 years. A nutritious fermented food usually made from soybeans, tempeh is high in protein and a great substitute for meat. It comes in a refrigerated rectangular cake and takes on the flavor of foods it is cooked with.

Serves 4

1 package TJ's Organic 3 Grain Tempeh
2 tablespoons water
2 red or green bell peppers
1 large sweet potato, diced, or use 9 ounces TJ's Sweet Potato Spears
⅓ teaspoon TJ's Crushed Garlic, or 1 clove garlic, minced
1 onion, chopped, or 1 cup TJ's Diced Onions
1 tablespoon curry powder
8 ounces TJ's Light Coconut Milk
½ cup fresh basil, chopped
2 tablespoons TJ's Reduced Sodium Soy Sauce or reduced sodium tamari
2 pouches frozen TJ's Brown Rice or 4 cups cooked brown rice

1. Spray a large nonstick skillet with cooking spray and heat to medium-high. Add the tempeh and sauté until the edges turn brown, about 5 minutes. Remove the tempeh and keep warm.
2. Add water to the skillet and then add the peppers, sweet potato, garlic and onion; sauté ten minutes. If the vegetables get too dry, add more water and stir.
3. Add the tempeh to the vegetables. Add curry powder, coconut milk, basil and soy sauce and cook over medium heat for about ten minutes.
4. While the curried tempeh is heating, heat the rice according to package directions.
5. Serve the curried tempeh over rice.

Per serving: 390 calories, 11 g fat, 0 mg cholesterol, 286 mg sodium, 58 g carbohydrate, 8.5 g fiber, 11 g protein

Options:
- Substitute tofu or chopped chicken for the tempeh.
- Substitute broccoli, cauliflower or other vegetables in place of peppers.

 *Gluten-free if you use tarmari in place of soy sauce

🌱 Vegan

Serve with:
Quick and Super-quick: Cauliflower with Curry Sauce (50 calories), page 166

Thai Coconut Curry

This easy vegetarian meal comes together in minutes, thanks to a convenient container of TJ's fresh Asian Stir Fry Vegetables, a jar of TJ's Curry Simmer Sauce, and TJ's cooked brown rice.

Serves 4

2 tablespoons water
1 package fresh TJ's Asian Stir Fry
   or frozen Stir Fry Vegetables
1 package TJ's Broccoli Florets or
   4 cups broccoli florets
⅔ cup TJ's Light Coconut Milk
½ cup Curry Simmer Sauce
1 teaspoon curry powder
1 (14 ounce) package TJ's Firm
   Tofu, chopped into ½-inch
   cubes
Zest of 1 lime
1 tablespoon lime juice
2 pouches frozen TJ's Brown Rice
   or 4 cups cooked brown rice
¼ cup chopped cilantro, optional

1. In a medium saucepan on medium-high heat, add water and vegetables and stir frequently, until vegetables are just tender, about 7 minutes.
2. Add coconut milk, simmer sauce and curry powder and simmer about 3 minutes. Add tofu and heat 2 to 3 more minutes.
3. Heat rice according to package directions.
4. Add lime zest and juice to the curry and serve over rice. Add cilantro, if desired.

Per serving: *335 calories, 9 g fat, 0 mg cholesterol, 273 mg sodium, 46 g carbohydrate, 6.3 g fiber, 13 g protein*

Options:
- Substitute 2 cups cooked edamame for tofu.
- Substitute 1 package frozen TJ's Stir Fry Vegetables in place of Asian Stir Fry.
- Substitute TJ's Yellow Thai Curry Simmer Sauce in place of Curry Simmer Sauce.
- Add 1 cup baby corn, drained and rinsed.

 Gluten-free

 Vegan

Serve with:
Quick: Butternut Squash Curry and Peanut Butter Soup (using TJ's Low Sodium Butternut Squash Soup) (137 calories), page 95
Super-quick: Cauliflower with Curry Sauce (50 calories), page 166

Baked Teriyaki Tofu Salad

This light, crunchy salad is easy to take to work or wherever you happen to be going. Package the wasabi peas separately and add them just before serving so they stay crunchy. This recipe is adapted from a similar one, Asian Chopped Salad, in *Vegetarian Times.*

Serves 4

1 (7 ounce) package TJ's Baked Tofu, Teriyaki flavor, cut into ½-inch cubes
1 red bell pepper, chopped
½ cup TJ's Wasabi Peas
1 English cucumber, chopped
1 teaspoon minced peeled fresh ginger or ¾ teaspoon bottled minced ginger
⅓ teaspoon TJ's Crushed Garlic, or 1 clove garlic, minced
¾ cup TJ's Sesame Soy Ginger Vinaigrette
3 scallions, sliced
¼ cup chopped fresh cilantro, optional

1. Place the tofu, red pepper, peas, and cucumber in a medium bowl and toss.
2. Combine ginger, garlic and dressing in a small bowl. Add to tofu and vegetables and toss to mix well.

Per serving: 216 calories, 4 g fat, 0 mg cholesterol, 733 mg sodium, 23 g carbohydrate, 3.6 g fiber, 11 g protein

Options:
- To lower sodium, replace tofu with 1 cup of edamame, or use firm or extra firm tofu.
- Substitute TJ's Asian Style Spicy Peanut Vinaigrette in place of Sesame Soy Ginger Vinaigrette.
- Add 3 cups of shredded cabbage.
- Add 3 cups of TJ's Broccoli Slaw.
- Add 1 tablespoon toasted sesame seeds.

 *Vegan if wasabi peas have no animal products (they are not on TJ's list of vegan foods but may be vegan)

Serve with:
Quick and Super-quick: TJ's Broccoli Slaw with Asian Style Spicy Peanut Vinaigrette, or raw cut-up vegetables including carrots and snap peas

Tofu and Broccoli in Peanut Sauce

If you were to make this dish all from scratch, it would take you a while to put it together. The combination of prepared peanut sauces with all of the other ingredients comes together to create a delicious higher protein dish with a respectable sodium count.

Serves 4

2 teaspoons water or vegetable broth

2 (12 ounce) bags TJ's Broccoli Florets or 8 cups broccoli florets

1 small red bell pepper, chopped

6 white or crimini mushrooms, sliced

½ cup TJ's Sugar Snap Peas, sliced in thirds

1 (14 ounce) package TJ's Firm Tofu, cubed

½ cup TJ's Satay Peanut Sauce

2 tablespoons natural style peanut butter, creamy or crunchy

3 tablespoons TJ's Asian Style Spicy Peanut Vinaigrette

¼ teaspoon red pepper flakes, optional

¼ cup TJ's Light Coconut Milk, optional

¼ cup chopped peanuts, optional

2 pouches frozen TJ's Brown Rice or 4 cups cooked brown rice

¼ cup chopped cilantro, optional

1. In a large nonstick skillet over medium-high heat, add water and sauté broccoli, red pepper, mushrooms, snap peas and tofu for 5 minutes.
2. Heat rice according to package directions.
3. Stir together peanut sauce, peanut butter and vinaigrette (add optional pepper flakes and coconut milk if desired) in a small bowl. Pour sauce over vegetables and tofu, and stir until blended. Reduce heat and simmer for 3 minutes. Serve over rice and top with cilantro, if desired.

Per serving: 276 calories, 11 g fat, 0 mg cholesterol, 386 mg sodium, 38 g carbohydrate, 6.7 g fiber, 21 g protein

Options:

- Substitute 2 packages fresh TJ's Asian Stir Fry or frozen TJ's Stir Fry Vegetables for broccoli, peppers, mushrooms and snap peas.
- Substitute snow peas for snap peas.
- Substitute rice noodles for rice.
- To reduce fat, reduce peanut butter to 1 tablespoon.

 Vegan

Serve with:

Quick: Spinach Salad with 2 tablespoons TJ's Peanut Vinaigrette (about 102 calories per serving), page 80

Super-quick: 2 cups frozen Hodgepodge cooked with ¼ teaspoon ginger and ⅓ teaspoon crushed garlic in a nonstick skillet with a teaspoon of toasted sesame oil or broth (140 calories/serving total if you use oil)

Grilled or Baked Teriyaki Tofu

Even those who claim that they don't like tofu want to know how to make this very simple recipe after they dare to taste it. Serve over Asian style vegetables and rice or noodles, or use as a sandwich filling or atop a green salad.

Serves 6

½ cup TJ's Soyaki Sauce or
    Teriyaki Sauce
1 (14 ounce) package TJ's Firm
    Tofu

1. Pour half of Soyaki Sauce into a 9 x 9-inch shallow pan.
2. Slice tofu into 3 horizontal slices and then in half, making 6 pieces. Place each piece on the Soyaki sauce.
3. Pour the other half of Soyaki Sauce over the tofu and marinate for 30 minutes.
4. Broil or grill tofu, turning over once for 2 or 3 minutes each side, or bake tofu at 350ºF, uncovered, for 40 minutes. If you want the tofu to be firmer, cook 10 to 15 minutes longer until desired firmness.

Per serving: *105 calories, 8.3 g fat, 0 mg cholesterol, 662 mg sodium, 9.3 g carbohydrate, 1.5 g fiber, 11 g protein*

Note: Unless all of the sauce is absorbed by the tofu, the actual amount of sodium will be less.

 Vegan

Serve with:
Quick: Ginger Garlic Broccoli (70 calories), page 168 and TJ's Frozen Brown Rice (160 calories per cup) or cooked Asian Rice Sticks
Super-quick: TJ's Fresh Asian Stir Fry vegetables cooked in a nonstick skillet with a little TJ's Soyaki Sauce and 1 cup heated frozen TJ's Brown Rice (160 calories/cup) or TJ's Rice Sticks (210 calories/serving)

Sweet Potato Chili or Soup

Here's a simple way to dress up a can of chili or black bean soup. You'll be pleasantly surprised by how easy it is to put this together after you taste it.

Serves 4

½ (12 ounce) package Sweet Potatoes Spears or 6 ounces sweet potatoes, peeled and chopped

1 (14.7 ounce) can TJ's Vegetarian Chili or Black Bean Soup

½ cup TJ's Mélange à Trois frozen peppers, Fire Roasted Bell Peppers and Onions, or roasted peppers in a jar, rinsed and chopped

½ teaspoon cumin

2 tablespoons red onion, diced

1 tablespoon lime juice

½ cup chopped cilantro

Plain low- or nonfat yogurt, optional

Cilantro Salad Dressing or salsa, optional

1. Cook sweet potatoes according to package directions.
2. Combine sweet potatoes, chili or soup, peppers, cumin and onion in a large saucepan. Cook for 7 to 8 minutes on medium heat or place in a microwave-safe bowl and microwave 2 to 3 minutes. Add lime juice, cilantro and optional items, if desired.

Per serving: 118 calories, 6 g fat, 0 mg cholesterol, 608 mg sodium, 44 g carbohydrate, 5.8 g fiber, 9 g protein

Options:
- Substitute butternut squash for sweet potatoes.
- Substitute turkey or chicken chili for a non-vegetarian version.
- Add shrimp for a non-vegetarian version.

 Gluten-free

🌱 Vegan (without optional yogurt)

Serve with:
Quick: Green salad with TJ's Cilantro Salad dressing and TJ's Cornbread. Save 100 calories and 12 grams of fat per serving by making the following substitution if using TJ's Cornbread Mix: use applesauce or low-fat or nonfat yogurt in place of the oil. Use the same substitution if you make it from scratch.

Super-quick: Green salad with TJ's Cilantro Salad Dressing and warm corn tortillas

Peanut-Tamarind Sweet Potato Curry

This is one of my favorite recipes from my *Quick and Healthy Meals from Trader Joe's* cookbook. The blend of ginger, chili, curry powder, peanut butter and tamarind melts in your mouth. Find tamarind paste in an Asian, Indian or Whole Foods market, or use lime juice to replace it. This recipe is adapted from one in *Vegetarian Times*.

Serves 4

2 tablespoons water

1 onion, chopped, or use 1 cup TJ's Diced Onions

1 ½ (12 ounce) packages TJ's Sweet Potato Spears, or 1 pound sweet potatoes, peeled and cubed

3 teaspoons freshly grated ginger or 2 teaspoons bottled minced ginger

1 jalapeño chili, seeded and minced

1 teaspoon curry powder

½ cup TJ's Organic Hearty Vegetable Broth

¾ cup orange juice

¼ cup crunchy peanut butter, natural style

1 tablespoon brown sugar

1 teaspoon tamarind paste or lime juice

½ teaspoon salt

1 pouch frozen TJ's Brown Rice, or 2 cups cooked brown rice

1. Heat water in skillet over medium-high heat. Add onions and cook until translucent, about 3 minutes.
2. Add sweet potatoes and cook 1 minute. Stir in ginger and jalapeño and cook 1 minute. Stir in curry powder and cook 1 minute more.
3. Add broth and orange juice, stir, cover and reduce heat to medium-low. Simmer for 10 minutes, or until sweet potatoes are soft.
4. Whisk together juice, peanut butter, brown sugar, tamarind paste and salt in a small bowl. Add to the sweet potatoes and bring to a simmer. Cook 5 minutes, or until sauce thickens. Serve over rice.

Per serving: *320 calories, 10 g fat, 0 mg cholesterol, 456 mg sodium, 52 g carbohydrate, 6.8 g fiber, 8 g protein*

Options:
- Substitute butternut squash for sweet potatoes.
- To increase protein, add lentils, tempeh, or tofu.
- For a non-vegetarian version, add shrimp or chicken.

 *Gluten-free if use gluten-free vegetable broth (TJ's Organic Hearty Vegetable Broth is gluten-free)

🌱 Vegan

Serve with:
Quick: Broccoli Peanut Slaw (90 calories), page 81
Super-quick: TJ's Honey Glazed Roasted Carrots and Parsnips (140 calories/serving)

Gnocchi Salad with Feta-Garlic Dressing

Gnocchi is a potato-based little dumpling. This higher-fiber meal made with cancer-fighting broccoli has lots of flavor. To make this dish even easier, use the suggestion in the options section and replace the dressing with TJ's Parmesan Ranch Dressing. This recipe is adapted from one on the Poor Girl Eats Well website, written by Kimberly Morales.

Serves 4

1 (18.5 ounce) package TJ's Whole Wheat Gnocchi
1 ½ cups TJ's Broccoli Florets
1 ½ cups frozen TJ's Petite Green Peas
1 medium red onion, thinly sliced

Feta-Garlic Dressing:
⅓ cup finely crumbled feta
½ cup nonfat plain yogurt
¼ cup nonfat milk
⅔ teaspoon TJ's Crushed Garlic or 2 large cloves of garlic, minced
1 tablespoon fresh lemon juice
Ground pepper, optional

1. Cook the gnocchi according to package instructions and add the broccoli 2 minutes before taking it off the stove. Remove the saucepan from the stove and add the peas.
2. Drain the gnocchi, broccoli and peas in a colander and rinse with cold water.
3. For the dressing, whisk together the feta, yogurt, milk, garlic and lemon juice in a medium bowl.
4. In a large bowl, combine the gnocchi, broccoli, peas, onions and the dressing. Toss together until everything is completely coated, cover and refrigerate (or set aside if you like your salads at room temperature). Garnish with extra ground black pepper, if desired.

Per serving: 300 calories, 2.7 g fat, 11 mg cholesterol, 510 mg sodium, 60 g carbohydrate, 9.75 g fiber, 9 g protein

Options:
- Serve on a bed of fresh spinach.
- Substitute TJ's Low Fat Parmesan Ranch Dressing and add a little Greek style yogurt to thicken it.
- Add cubed tofu, lentils or cooked chicken to add protein.

Serve with:
Quick: Green salad with raw or cooked vegetables and Fat Free Balsamic Vinaigrette
Super-quick: Sliced tomatoes with a little olive oil and balsamic vinegar, or TJ's Fat Free Balsamic Vinaigrette and fresh mozzarella

Quinoa, Mango and Black Bean Salad

Quinoa (pronounced kee-no-wha or keen-wha) is actually a high protein grain-like seed. It cooks similarly to rice and can even be cooked in a rice cooker. The texture is lighter but can be used in any dish calling for rice or grains. Toasting before cooking enhances its flavor. This recipe is adapted from one in *Eating Well* magazine.

Serves 4

2 cups water
1 cup uncooked TJ's Quinoa or
    4 cups cooked quinoa
½ cup orange juice
½ cup chopped fresh cilantro
4 tablespoons TJ's Seasoned
    Rice Vinegar
2 teaspoons TJ's Toasted Sesame
    Oil
2 teaspoons minced fresh ginger
    or 1 ½ teaspoons bottled ginger
    or ginger paste
2 tablespoons fresh lime juice
¼ teaspoon salt, optional
2 cups frozen TJ's Mango Chunks
    or fresh mango
2 small red bell peppers, diced
1 (15 ounce) can TJ's Black Beans,
    drained and rinsed
4 scallions, thinly sliced

1. Toast quinoa in a dry medium saucepan over medium heat, stirring often for 4 to 6 minutes or until it begins to crackle or pop. Rinse in a fine sieve or place cheesecloth over a colander and rinse and drain. Cook in water according to package directions.
2. While quinoa is cooking, combine orange juice, cilantro, rice vinegar, oil, ginger, salt, if using, cayenne and lime juice in a medium-size bowl. Add mango, red peppers, beans and scallions. Stir well.
3. Add quinoa and toss to combine. Chill for 2 hours before serving.

Per serving: 354 calories, 4.8 g fat, 0 mg cholesterol, 287 mg sodium, 69 g carbohydrate, 11 g fiber, 7.4 g protein

Options:
- Substitute 4 cups frozen TJ's Quinoa Duo instead of cooking 1 cup quinoa. (Eliminate water if skipping this step.)
- Add 2 tablespoons TJ's Smoky, Spicy, Peach Salsa or TJ's Papaya Mango Salsa.
- Add chopped cooked chicken or shrimp for a non-vegetarian version and to add protein.

 Gluten-free

 Vegan

Serve with:
Quick and Super-quick: Serve salad on a bed of lettuce or fresh spinach with TJ's Low Sodium Butternut Squash Soup (70 calories/cup)

Sweet Potato Black Bean Salad

The Center for Science in the Public Interest (CSPI) ranked the sweet potato number one in nutrition of all vegetables. Besides being a good source of dietary fiber and complex carbohydrates, sweet potatoes also have almost twice the recommended daily allowance of vitamin A, 42 percent of the recommended dosage for vitamin C, four times the RDA for beta carotene and other antioxidants. I sometimes eat cooked sweet potatoes for dessert.

Serves 4

1½ (12 ounce) packages TJ's Sweet Potato Spears or Cubes (Cubes are sold seasonally) or 1 pound sweet potatoes, peeled and chopped

1 (15 ounce can) black beans, drained and rinsed

1 cup frozen TJ's Fire Roasted Peppers and Onions, chopped

1 cup frozen TJ's Mango Chunks, each piece chopped into fourths

¾ cup watercress, chopped

½ cup chopped red or purple onion

¾ teaspoon chili powder

2 tablespoons extra virgin olive oil

1 clove garlic

2 tablespoons red wine vinegar

¼ teaspoon hot pepper sauce

8 cups lettuce

1. Cook sweet potatoes according to package directions.
2. Combine all the ingredients in a large bowl. Toss to blend. Cover and let stand at room temperature for 15 minutes or refrigerate for 1 hour. To serve, spoon onto fresh greens.

Per serving: 290 calories, 7 g fat, 0 mg cholesterol, 370 mg sodium, 47 g carbohydrate, 10 g fiber, 8 g protein

Options:
- Use cilantro in place of watercress.
- Add cumin and lime juice to taste.

🚫 *Gluten-free if hot sauce is gluten-free (TJ's Jalapeño Hot Sauce and Chili Pepper Sauce are gluten-free)

🌱 Vegan

Serve with:
Quick and Super-quick: TJ's Low Sodium Tomato and Roasted Red Pepper Soup with ¼ teaspoon cumin and a dollop of low-fat yogurt (110 calories/cup)

Warm Lentil and Butternut Squash Salad with Tahini Sauce

Steamed lentils and peeled and cubed butternut squash make this delicious salad a breeze to put together. I served this to friends on New Years Eve and one of the guys, a gourmet cook, said he would eat healthier food more often if it tasted this good. How's that for an endorsement? Find the Tahini Sauce in the refrigerated section by the hummus and salsa. This recipe is adapted from a recipe by Molly Wizenberg's Orangette website.

Serves 4

TJ's Extra Virgin Olive Oil Spray
2 ½ (12 ounce) packages TJ's Cut Butternut Squash or 2 pounds butternut squash
⅔ teaspoon TJ's Crushed Garlic or 2 cloves, chopped
1 teaspoon ground cumin
Pinch of salt, optional
¼ teaspoon freshly ground pepper
½ teaspoon red chili pepper flakes
½ teaspoon ground allspice, freshly ground if possible
1 tablespoon lemon juice

Sauce:

¼ teaspoon TJ's Crushed Garlic or not quite 1 clove, minced
4 tablespoons TJ's Tahini Sauce
2 cups TJ's Steamed Lentils or 2 cups cooked lentils
¼ medium red onion, finely chopped
¼ cup coarsely chopped parsley (or cilantro) leaves
½ teaspoon sumac, lemon pepper or paprika

1. Preheat oven to 425ºF.
2. Spray a large baking sheet with cooking spray and add butternut squash, garlic, cumin, salt, if using, pepper, pepper flakes and allspice. Stir butternut squash and spices until they are blended. Spray with olive oil spray and roast for about 15 minutes or until squash is tender when pierced with a fork.
3. Place lemon juice, garlic and tahini sauce in a small bowl and stir.
4. To assemble the salad, gently toss the lentils, the warm roasted squash, red onion and parsley in a serving bowl, along with most of the dressing. Serve the remaining tahini dressing at the table.

Per serving: 260 calories, 5.2 g fat, 0 mg cholesterol, 384 mg sodium, 45.6 g carbohydrate, 15.6 g fiber, 13 g protein

Option:
Substitute garbanzo beans in place of lentils and cilantro in place of parsley.

 Gluten-free

 Vegan

Serve with: Quick and Super-quick: Green salad with TJ's Low Fat Parmesan Ranch dressing, or steamed green beans or asparagus

Curried Lentil Salad

If lentils are not part of your regular diet, consider adding a few dishes to your repertoire when you are menu planning. They are high in fiber and an excellent source of protein if you combine them with rice or whole grains. They are an important source of B vitamins, especially B3, essential for both a healthy nervous system and digestive system. Also high in iron, zinc and calcium, lentils are a good replacement for red meat. Besides being so good for you, this is a great-tasting salad. The recipe is adapted from one that appeared in *Moosewood Restaurant Low Fat Favorites*.

Serves 4

2 ½ cups TJ's Steamed Lentils or
   2 ½ cups cooked lentils
1 cup finely chopped green
   bell peppers
1 cup finely chopped celery
1 cup finely chopped red onions

Dressing:
½ cup plain nonfat Greek style
   yogurt
3 tablespoons TJ's Mango Ginger
   Chutney
1 ½ teaspoons curry powder
2 teaspoons finely minced red
   onion
⅔ teaspoon TJ's Crushed Garlic or
   2 garlic cloves, minced
Juice from ½ lime
¼ teaspoon salt, optional
⅓ cup chopped fresh cilantro

1. Combine lentils, green peppers, celery and red onions in a medium bowl.
2. In a small bowl, combine the dressing ingredients, except the cilantro, and stir into the lentils. Fold in the cilantro. Serve at room temperature.

Per serving: 217 calories, 0 g fat, 0 mg cholesterol, 350 mg sodium, 36 g carbohydrate,11.5 g fiber, 14.4 g protein

Options:
- Substitute jicama for celery.
- Add 1 cup brown rice or wild rice and increase the Greek style yogurt to ⅔ cup.

 Gluten-free

Serve with:
Quick: Indian Spiced Couscous (255 calories), page 171 or Cauliflower with Curry Sauce (50 calories), page 166
Super-quick: frozen TJ's Biryani (170 calories)

Butternut Squash and Black Bean Burrito

This recipe originally called for sweet potatoes. Did you know that even though butternut squash and sweet potatoes are both good sources of beta carotene and vitamin A, butternut squash has significantly fewer calories? Per cup, butternut squash has about 100 calories less. Use it as a substitute in other recipes calling for sweet potatoes when you want to reduce calories. You may need to add a bit more seasoning if you are using butternut squash, depending on your palate, as sweet potatoes are a bit sweeter.

Serves 3

1½ (12 ounce) packages TJ's
   Butternut Squash, or 1 pound
   cooked butternut squash
1 teaspoon water
¼ medium red or yellow onion,
   chopped
⅓ teaspoon TJ's Crushed Garlic or
   1 clove, minced
¼ teaspoon minced green chili
¼ teaspoon ground cumin
¼ teaspoon ground coriander
⅛ teaspoon cayenne pepper,
   optional
1 (15 ounce) can black beans,
   rinsed and drained
4 TJ's Whole Wheat Tortillas
1 cup fresh spinach, chopped
¼ cup cilantro, optional
1 teaspoon lime juice, optional
Salsa, optional
Light or nonfat sour cream,
   optional

1. Cook butternut squash
   according to package
   directions, or use cooked
   butternut squash.

2. Heat water in a nonstick skillet over medium-high heat and add onion, garlic and chili. Cook for about 2 minutes. Add cumin, coriander and cayenne pepper, if using. Cook another 2 minutes, stirring frequently.
3. Add black beans and stir until heated through.
4. Heat tortillas in the oven or the microwave.
5. To assemble burritos, fill each warm tortilla with the black bean filling. Add chopped spinach and cilantro, if using. Top with salsa and low-fat sour cream, if desired.

Per serving: 321 calories, 0.6 g fat, 0 mg cholesterol, 336 mg sodium, 72 g carbohydrate, 14 g fiber, 13.8 g protein

Options:
- Use sweet potatoes in place of butternut squash.
- Omit the tortilla and eat the filling by itself, on a salad, or as a side dish.

Vegan (without optional sour cream, or use soy yogurt in place of sour cream)

*Gluten-free if you use TJ's Brown Rice Tortillas in place of whole wheat tortillas or other grain options.

Serve with:
Quick and Super-quick: Green salad with raw or cooked vegetables and TJ's Cilantro Salad Dressing

Lentil Pasta with Cinnamon and Tomatoes

Here's another flavorful, convenient way to get the many health benefits lentils offer into your diet. Adding cinnamon adds a whole new dimension in this dish.

Sometimes family members can be resistant to eating whole wheat pasta. If that is the case, try mixing white and whole wheat pastas together. Over time, increase the ratio of whole wheat pasta. The same idea can work with brown and white rice.

Serves 4

1 onion, chopped, or 1 cup TJ's Diced Onions

1 tablespoon water

1 teaspoon TJ's Crushed Garlic or 3 cloves of garlic, crushed or finely chopped

½ teaspoon ground cinnamon

2 cups TJ's Steamed Lentils

1 (14 ounce) can TJ's Diced & No Salt Added Tomatoes

2 tablespoons roughly chopped fresh basil or 1 teaspoon of dried basil or oregano

¼ teaspoon salt, optional

¼ teaspoon freshly ground black pepper, optional

8 ounces dry TJ's Whole Wheat Rotelle

1. In a nonstick large saucepan, gently sauté the onion in the water until translucent, about 3 minutes. Add the garlic and cinnamon and stir for a minute.

2. Add the lentils, tomatoes and basil or oregano. Add the salt and pepper, if using, and serve over the pasta.

Per serving: 361 calories, 1.5 g fat, 0 mg cholesterol, 352 mg sodium, 87 g carbohydrate, 14.25 g fiber, 18 g protein

Options:

- Add 1 teaspoon of turmeric and cumin and/or a dash of cayenne to add flavor.
- Add chickpeas.
- To lower carbohydrates, use less pasta.
- Substitute rice, quinoa or other grains in place of pasta.

🚫 *Gluten-free if you use gluten-free pasta such as rice pasta available at Trader Joe's or other grain options listed above.

🌱 Vegan

Serve with:

Quick and Super-quick: Green salad with cooked or raw vegetables and TJ's Fat Free Balsamic Vinaigrette

Chapter 13:

Simple Sides

In this section, you will find some delicious and simple recipes to add color, variety and nutrients to your plate. They offer the perfect opportunity to increase your intake of vegetables and fiber. In the cases when you don't have time or energy to put one together, I have included a list of healthy prepared side dish options offered by Trader Joe's on page 174 to 175.

Brussels Sprouts with Garlic and Balsamic Vinegar

I have always liked these compact little cabbages but I may be in the minority. If you are one of those who has steered clear of them, I hope you will give this recipe a try as Brussels sprouts are among the family of cruciferous vegetables, known for their cancer-preventing nutrients and antioxidants. This recipe is adapted from one by Sam Zien, The Cooking Guy.

Serves 4

¾ (16 ounce) package fresh or frozen TJ's Brussels Sprouts, trimmed of outer leaves and cut in quarters, or use fresh small Brussels sprouts, trimmed and cut in half

⅔ teaspoon TJ's Crushed Garlic or 2 cloves garlic, crushed

1 tablespoon balsamic vinegar

1 tablespoon brown sugar

½ teaspoon red pepper flakes

½ tablespoon extra virgin olive oil

1. Cook Brussels sprouts according to package directions. If using TJ's package, trim Brussels sprouts after they are cooked.
2. Heat olive oil and garlic in a small skillet on medium heat until fragrant, but do not burn.
3. Add Brussels sprouts and pepper flakes and stir until the Brussels sprouts begin to brown, about 2 minutes.
4. Add balsamic vinegar and brown sugar. Stir for a minute, remove from the heat, and serve warm.

Per serving: *53 calories, 5.8 g fat, 0 mg cholesterol, 2 mg sodium, 17 g carbohydrate, 2.8 g fiber, 2.8 g protein*

 *Gluten-free if your balsamic vinegar is gluten-free

 Vegan

Lemony Asparagus with Parsley

This recipe may be a nice change from the way you normally serve asparagus. Asparagus is low in calories (less than 4 calories per spear), an excellent source of folic acid (which is necessary for blood cell formation, growth and prevention of liver disease) and gives us lots of other vitamins and minerals. This recipe is adapted from one in *Cooking Light Super Fast Suppers*.

Serves 4

¾ (12 ounce) package TJ's
   Asparagus Spears (36) or
   ½ pound asparagus,
   diagonally-sliced
1 teaspoon extra virgin olive oil
2 tablespoons finely chopped
   fresh flat-leaf parsley
1 tablespoon lemon juice
¼ teaspoon salt
¼ teaspoon freshly ground black
   pepper

1. Steam asparagus over medium-
   high heat until tender-crisp,
   about 3 minutes.
2. Place asparagus in a medium
   bowl. Stir in oil, parsley, lemon
   juice, salt and pepper.

Per serving: 45 calories, 1.4 g fat, 0 mg cholesterol, 151 mg sodium, 5 g carbohydrate, 2.2 g fiber, 2.4 g protein

🚫 Gluten-free

🌱 Vegan

Broccoli with Lemon Zest

My friend Dawn brought this incredible broccoli dish to our book group and we devoured it. She is one of those cooks that adds a little of this and a little of that. This is an approximation of what she used. You can find Asian chili paste and hot mustard at the grocery store or Asian market.

Serves 8

3 (12 ounce) bags TJ's Broccoli Florets or about 12 cups broccoli florets (it seems like a lot but they get smaller when they're cooked)

1 teaspoon Asian chili paste

1 teaspoon Chinese hot mustard

1 teaspoon tamari or TJ's Reduced Sodium Soy Sauce

1 teaspoon prepared TJ's Horseradish

Zest and juice of 2 lemons

1 teaspoon TJ's White Balsamic Vinegar or rice vinegar

2 teaspoons extra virgin olive oil

1. Steam broccoli according to package directions until fork-tender but not mushy.
2. In a small bowl, whisk the rest of the ingredients together and pour over cooked broccoli. Serve warm or at room temperature.

Per serving: 38 calories, 1.2 g fat, 0 mg cholesterol, 162 mg sodium, 4.4 g carbohydrate, 1 g fiber, 1.5 g protein

 *Gluten-free if you use tamari in place of soy sauce.

 Vegan

Cauliflower with Curry Sauce

Cauliflower is a cruciferous vegetable. Cruciferous vegetables may help lower your risk of getting cancer, as well as offering other health benefits. Be sure to avoid overcooking cauliflower, as it can become mushy and flavorless when overcooked. Try this sauce with broccoli as well.

Serves 4

1 (12 ounce) package TJ's Cauliflower Florets or 1 small cauliflower, cut into florets
½ cup low-fat plain yogurt
3 tablespoons TJ's Yellow Thai Curry Sauce
⅛ teaspoon red curry paste, optional

Steam cauliflower according to package directions. Mix yogurt and curry sauce together in a small bowl. Pour sauce over cauliflower.

Per serving: 50 calories, 1.3 g fat, 1.8 mg cholesterol, 192 mg sodium, 27.2 g carbohydrate, 1.67 g fiber, 3 g protein

Option:
Serve as an appetizer at room temperature and dip cauliflower florets into curry yogurt sauce.

 Gluten-free

 Vegetarian

Marmalade-Glazed Carrots

An easy way to add a bit of flavor to cooked carrots. Lightly cooked carrots can be easier to digest for some people than raw carrots. If you find that to be true for you, make sure you give this recipe a try.

Serves 4

¾ package (16 ounces) TJ's Cut and Peeled Carrots or 3 cups baby carrots
¼ cup water
¼ cup orange marmalade
4 lemon wedges

In a large nonstick skillet, heat water and cook the carrots over medium-high heat about 7 minutes, or until carrots are crisp-tender. Or steam them. Add the marmalade and stir until the carrots are well coated and shiny. Serve with lemon wedges.

Per serving: *48 calories, 0 g fat, 0 mg cholesterol, 65 mg sodium, 11 g carbohydrate, 2 g fiber, 1 g protein*

Options:
- Add a pinch of cinnamon and nutmeg and leave out the lemon.
- Cook carrots in vegetable broth and add ¼ teaspoon cumin and ¼ cup white wine.

 Gluten-free

Vegan

Ginger-Garlic Broccoli

This recipe is especially good when accompanying an Asian-inspired entrée.

Serves 6

1 ½ teaspoons minced fresh
    ginger or 1 teaspoon bottled
    minced ginger
⅓ teaspoon TJ's Crushed Garlic or
    1 clove garlic, minced
1 tablespoon TJ's Reduced Sodium
    Soy Sauce or tamari
1 teaspoon TJ's Toasted Sesame Oil
1 tablespoon fresh lemon juice
2 ½ (12 ounce) packages TJ's
    Broccoli Florets or 2 pounds
    broccoli florets and peeled and
    sliced stalks
1 tablespoon toasted sesame
    seeds, optional
Freshly ground black pepper

1. In a small bowl, whisk together
   the ginger, garlic, soy sauce,
   sesame oil and lemon juice.
2. Steam broccoli until tender-
   crisp, 4 to 6 minutes. Place the
   broccoli in a serving bowl and
   toss with the sauce. Sprinkle
   with sesame seeds, if desired,
   and add the pepper.

Per serving: *60 calories, 2 g fat, 0 mg cholesterol, 118 mg sodium, 8 g carbohydrate, 5 g fiber, 3 g protein*

Options:
- Substitute TJ's Sesame Soy Ginger Vinaigrette in place of the sauce.
- Substitute bok choy, chard or kale for the broccoli.

*Gluten-free if you use tamari in place of soy sauce

Vegan

Kale and Quinoa Pilaf

Here are two powerhouse ingredients in one recipe. If you are new to quinoa, you are in for a treat. Besides tasting great, it contains a balanced set of essential amino acids, making it an unusually complete protein source among plant foods. It is also a good source of dietary fiber as well as other nutrients. This recipe is adapted from one that appeared on the Food 52 website.

Serves 4

1 cup quinoa
2 cups water
½ (12 ounce) package TJ's Kale chopped into 1-inch lengths, or fresh spinach
1 Meyer lemon or ½ regular lemon, zested and juiced
2 green onions, minced
1 tablespoon extra virgin olive oil
¼ cup crumbled goat cheese or feta cheese
3 tablespoons pine nuts, optional
Salt and pepper, optional

1. Toast quinoa in a large nonstick skillet over medium heat for 4 to 5 minutes or until the quinoa is light brown and begins to pop.
2. Bring the water to a boil in a medium pot over high heat. Add the quinoa. Cover, lower the heat and simmer for 10 minutes. Add kale on top of the quinoa and cover. Simmer for 5 minutes. Take off the heat and let steam for 5 more minutes.
3. While the quinoa rests, combine half of the lemon juice, all of the lemon zest, scallions, olive oil and goat cheese in a large bowl.
4. Fluff the kale and quinoa and add it into the bowl. Toss to combine, seasoning with salt and pepper if needed. Taste and add the remaining lemon juice, if desired.

Per serving: 218 calories, 9 g fat, 2.5 mg cholesterol, 65 mg sodium, 30 g carbohydrate, 4.5 g fiber, 8.25 g protein

Option:
Cook quinoa in reduced sodium chicken or vegetable broth for added flavor.

Note: Unless quinoa is rinsed and/or toasted, it may have a bitter taste from its natural coating, which has been rinsed considerably by the time it gets to our markets, but which may still exist in small amounts.

 Gluten-free

 Vegetarian

Butternut Squash Curried Rice

This super-simple side dish makes a great accompaniment to a curry flavored entrée or salad. My cooking class participants are amazed at how delicious yet simple this is. Check out the options below on how to expand this side dish into an entrée.

Serves 4

1 pouch frozen TJ's Brown Rice or
   2 cups cooked brown rice
1 cup TJ's Butternut Squash Soup
½ cup TJ's Curry Simmer Sauce
Dash of curry powder or dab of
   red curry paste, optional

Combine the rice, soup and simmer sauce in a medium saucepan and heat for 6 to 8 minutes or place in a microwave-safe bowl and heat for 2 minutes.

Per serving: *128 calories, 2 g fat, 0 mg cholesterol, 336 mg sodium, 25 g carbohydrate, 2 g fiber, 3.6 g protein*

Options:

- Add lentils or cubed tofu and serve over wilted spinach to make this a complete meal.
- Add cauliflower and garbanzo beans.
- Substitute TJ's Yellow Thai Curry Sauce in place of simmer sauce.
- Add cooked cubed butternut squash.
- Add more soup and serve as a spicy soup.
- Substitute TJ's Low Sodium Butternut Squash Soup for TJ's Butternut Squash Soup to lower sodium.

 Gluten-free

 Vegan

Indian Spiced Couscous

Couscous is a precooked pasta and it only takes a few minutes to bring it back to life. It takes on the flavors of the ingredients you cook it with. This recipe is adapted from one in *Cooking Light Super Fast Suppers.*

Serves 4

2 cups water

½ cup raisins or a mixture of
   dried fruit

1 medium carrot, chopped finely

2 teaspoons extra virgin olive oil

¼ teaspoon salt

½ teaspoon freshly ground
   black pepper

½ teaspoon ground turmeric

Dash of ground cardamom

½ teaspoon ground cinnamon

1 cup TJ's Whole Wheat Couscous,
   uncooked

6 tablespoon thinly sliced green
   onions

1. Combine water, raisins, carrot, olive oil, salt, pepper, turmeric, cardamom and cinnamon in a medium-sized saucepan and bring to a boil over medium-high heat.
2. Stir in couscous and return to a boil. Cover the saucepan and reduce the heat to low. Simmer 2 minutes, or until water is absorbed.
3. Remove couscous from the heat and add green onions. Cover and let stand 5 minutes. Fluff with a fork before serving.

Per serving: *255 calories, 3.1 g fat, 0 mg cholesterol, 163 mg sodium, 51 g carbohydrate, 6.6 g fiber, 12.8 g protein*

Option:
Add cooked chicken, garbanzo beans or cubed tofu to serve this dish as an entrée.

 Vegan

Curried Quinoa Greens with Coconut Dressing

Besides being high in vitamin A and C and many other vitamins and minerals important to our health, kale is a good source of calcium. I add chopped kale to many dishes such as soups and stews. I even add it to my scrambled eggs some mornings.

This is a light, colorful side dish and goes well with fish or chicken with similar flavors. If you only have regular coconut milk, dilute it 50% with water and you'll have light coconut milk. Freeze whatever you have left over in labeled small containers or in an ice cube tray to be transferred to a freezer bag for future use.

Serves 4

1 cup TJ's Quinoa, uncooked
2 ¾ cups TJ's Organic Hearty
   Vegetable Broth
3 cups kale, stems removed and
chopped into small pieces
1 teaspoon curry powder
3 tablespoons TJ's Light Coconut
   Milk
2 teaspoons fresh lime juice
¼ teaspoon curry powder
¼ teaspoon agave nectar
⅓ cup peanuts, dry roasted/
unsalted, optional

1. In a large nonstick skillet (with a lid) over medium heat, toast quinoa for 5 to 6 minutes, stirring frequently until quinoa begins to brown and pop.

2. Add the broth, kale, curry powder and cover. Increase the heat and bring the mixture to a boil. Lower the heat and simmer until the moisture is absorbed and the kale is tender, about 15 minutes. Remove the skillet from the heat and place the mixture into a medium-size bowl.

3. Whisk together the coconut milk, lime juice, curry powder and agave nectar in a small bowl; pour it over the quinoa mixture and toss to combine. Serve warm or chilled. Add peanuts before serving, if desired.

Per serving: 209 calories, 4.45 g fat, 0 mg cholesterol, 258 mg sodium, 38 g carbohydrate, 6 g fiber, 8 g protein

Options:
• Use spinach in place of kale but add it towards the end of the 15 minutes of simmering.
• Use broccoli in place of kale.
• Use maple syrup or honey in place of agave nectar or leave it out.

 Gluten-free

 Vegan

Brown Rice Pilaf

The chicken broth used in this recipe comes in slim concentrated tubes (inside a box), allowing more flavor with less liquid and works well in this simple side dish recipe.

Serves 2

4 tablespoons water

2 small yellow onions, chopped or use 1 cup TJ's Diced Onions

2 teaspoons TJ's Crushed Garlic or 6 garlic cloves, minced

2 pouches frozen TJ's Brown Rice, or 4 cups cooked brown rice

4 packets TJ's Savory Broth Chicken Flavor Reduced Sodium Liquid Concentrate, dissolved in ½ cup warm water

Freshly ground black pepper

1. In a small nonstick skillet, heat water over medium-high heat. Add onion and garlic and cook, stirring, until the onion is translucent, about 3 minutes.
2. Add rice and dissolved broth and stir until combined. Simmer until water is absorbed, stirring often, about 5 minutes. Sprinkle with pepper and serve.

__Per serving:__ 194 calories, 2.8 g fat, 0 mg cholesterol, 374 mg sodium, 41 g carbohydrates, 3.4 g fiber, 4.5 g protein

 Dairy-free

 Gluten-free

Trader Joe's 'Heat and Eat' Prepared Grain-Based Side Dishes

If you don't have time or just don't feel like making your own side dishes sometimes, these 'heat and eat' dishes couldn't be easier to prepare. Substitute chicken or vegetable broth for oil and save 120 calories and 14 grams of fat/tablespoon if the directions on the package ask you to add a tablespoon of oil or butter during preparation.

These dishes make great side dishes for chicken, lean beef, fish or vegetarian entrées. Many of them can be the base for an entrée by adding a protein such as chicken, fish, lean beef, beans, tempeh or tofu. They have been selected because they are well seasoned, are of reasonable serving size, have 5 grams or less of fat and 500 mg or less of sodium. Products change often at Trader Joe's and these may or may not be available. Check my Web site: www.HealthyTraderJoes.com for updates to this list.

Frozen

Baingan Bhart (serves 3) Eggplant curry
Per serving: 100 calories, 4.5 g fat,
0 mg cholesterol, 210 mg sodium,
12 g carbohydrate, 1 g fiber, 2 g protein

Biryani (serves 3) Indian curried rice with peas, red pepper, apples raisins and spices
Per serving: 170 calories, 0 g fat,
0 mg cholesterol, 650 mg sodium,
36 g carbohydrate, 2 g fiber, 4 g protein

Fettuccine with Mushrooms (serves 3) Fettuccine mushrooms and sauce
Per serving: 150 calories, 5 g fat,
35 mg cholesterol, 350 mg sodium,
22 g carbohydrate, 2 g fiber, 6 g protein

Grilled Eggplant and Zucchini Mélange (serves 4) Eggplant, zucchini and mozzarella
Per serving: 70 calories, 2.5 g fat,
5 mg cholesterol, 310 mg sodium,
8 g carbohydrate, 0.5 g fiber, 4 g protein

Gnocchialla Sorrentina (serves 3) Gnocchi, tomatoes and mozzarella
Per serving: 170 calories, 2.5 g fat,
5 mg cholesterol, 500 mg sodium,
30 g carbohydrate, 3 g fiber, 6 g protein

Mushroom Risotto (serves 3) Rice, mushrooms and sauce
Per serving: 150 calories, 3 g fat,
5 mg cholesterol, 350 mg sodium,
28 g carbohydrate, 0 g fiber, 3 g protein

Penne Arrabbiata (serves 3) Pasta and red sauce

Per serving: 200 calories, 6 g fat,
0 mg cholesterol, 470 mg sodium,
39 g carbohydrate, 3 g fiber, 7 g protein

Penne Pepperonata (serves 4.5)
Pasta, red bell peppers and cream sauce

Per serving: 200 calories, 4.5 g fat,
10 mg cholesterol, 190 mg sodium,
35 g carbohydrate, 3 g fiber, 7 g protein

Polenta Provencale (serves 4) Polenta with spinach, peas, tomatoes, cream and herbs de Provence

Per serving:130 calories, 7 g fat,
20 mg cholesterol, 280 mg sodium,
13 g carbohydrate, 3 g fiber, 4 g protein

Quinoa Duo with Vegetable Mélange (serves 3) Quinoa with zucchini, sweet potato and flavorings

Per serving: 220 calories, 6 g fat,
0 mg cholesterol, 260 mg sodium,
36 g carbohydrate, 4 g fiber, 6 g protein

Rice Medley (serves 6) Brown rice, red rice and black barley

Per serving: 200 calories, 1.5 g fat,
0 mg cholesterol, 0 mg sodium,
42 g carbohydrate, 4 g fiber, 5 g protein

Soycatash (serves 5) Corn, edamame and red peppers

Per serving: 100 calories, 3 g fat,
0 mg cholesterol, 0 mg sodium,
14 g carbohydrate, 4 g fiber, 6 g protein

Chapter 14:

Slow Cooker Recipes

Would you like to come home to a delicious home-cooked meal at the end of the day? Many people have rediscovered slow cookers and use them to solve the "What's for dinner tonight?" dilemma. These lower-calorie recipes are from my *Simmering Solutions, Healthy Slow Cooker Recipes* cookbook, which includes my popular Chicken Tortilla Soup and Mexican-Flavored Beef Stew. Get more information at my website: www.HealthyTraderJoes.com.

You can use a timer (such as the one you may use to have your lights come on at a certain time) to delay the start of cooking for up to two hours. Your slow cooker also may have a delay feature built in. Or, cook during the night, refrigerate the meal and heat it upon your return at the end of the day.

Chicken Cacciatore

Serve this tasty Italian chicken dish with, what else? Pasta!

Serves 6

1 medium onion, chopped, or
   1 cup TJ's Diced Onions
1 green bell pepper, seeded and
   chopped
1 clove garlic, minced
1 (15 ounce) can whole
   tomatoes, undrained; or 1 can
   TJ's Diced Tomatoes,
   undrained
1 (4 ounce) can sliced
   mushrooms, rinsed
2 teaspoons tomato paste
½ cup fresh parsley, minced
1 bay leaf
¼ teaspoon ground thyme
½ teaspoon dried basil,
   crumbled
1 teaspoon salt
Dash freshly ground black pepper
4 skinless, boneless chicken
   breast halves, about 24 ounces
1 (16 ounce) package TJ's
   Organic Whole Wheat Rotelle,
   or other pasta
1 tablespoon minced pimento
Fresh Parmesan cheese, grated

1. Place the onion, green pepper, garlic, tomatoes, mushrooms, tomato paste, parsley, bay leaf, thyme, basil, salt and pepper in a 3 ½-quart slow cooker. Add chicken pieces, pushing down into liquid to thoroughly coat.
2. Cover and cook on LOW for 7 to 9 hours. Add pimento and stir. Remove bay leaf before serving.
3. Cook rotelle according to package directions and drain.
4. Remove bay leaf from chicken and add pimento and stir. Serve chicken over pasta and sprinkle with Parmesan.

Per serving: 380 calories, 6.2 g fat, 65 mg cholesterol, 400 mg sodium, 62 g carbohydrate, 9.7 g fiber, 32 g protein

Options:
- Substitute 1 teaspoon dried rosemary and ½ teaspoon dried marjoram for ground thyme and dried basil.
- Substitute TJ's Low Sodium Chicken Broth and TJ's Diced & No Salt Added Tomatoes to lower sodium.

Awesome Turkey Chili

The unexpected ingredients of cocoa powder and beer give this chili its deep flavor. When selecting ground turkey, remember that the amount of fat in ground turkey varies, depending on the proportion of dark and light meat. For a lower-fat version of this recipe, use extra-lean turkey breast. The label will indicate that it has about 1.5 grams of fat per 4 ounces versus lean, which has about 8 grams of fat.

Serves 10

1 tablespoon extra virgin olive oil

2 large onions, chopped or
2 cups TJ's Diced Onions

1 ⅓ teaspoons TJ's Crushed
Garlic or 4 large garlic cloves, minced

2 pounds lean ground turkey or chicken

¼ cup chili powder

1 tablespoon ground cumin

2 teaspoons dried oregano, crumbled

2 teaspoons unsweetened cocoa powder

½ teaspoon cayenne powder or to taste

Salt and freshly ground black pepper to taste

2 (15 ounce) cans TJ's Diced Tomatoes, undrained

2 tablespoons tomato paste

2 (15 ounce) cans pinto or kidney beans, drained and rinsed

1 (12 ounce) bottle dark beer

½ cup TJ's Chicken Broth

1 bay leaf

1. Heat oil in a nonstick skillet on medium heat. Add the onions and cook for about 3 minutes, stirring occasionally.
2. Add the garlic and transfer onion and garlic to a bowl.
3. Increase the heat to high and cook the ground turkey until lightly browned. Pour off the excess fat.
4. Place the onions, garlic and turkey in a 3 ½ to 5-quart slow cooker. Add the remaining ingredients and cook on LOW for 6 to 8 hours. Remove bay leaf before serving.

Per serving: 280 calories, 10 g fat, 64 mg cholesterol, 520 mg sodium*, 22 g carbohydrates, 5.5 g fiber, 34 g protein

* Rinsing the beans will reduce the sodium by at least one third. Reduce sodium further by substituting TJ's Low Sodium Chicken Broth (70 mg/cup) for chicken broth. (520 mg sodium reflects the rinsed beans)

 Dairy-free

Curry Spiced Lentils and Spinach

A vegetarian dish that is easy to take for lunch in a microwave-safe container.

Serves 6

3 teaspoons curry powder

1 teaspoon ground cumin

2 teaspoons ground ginger

½ teaspoon turmeric

½ teaspoon cayenne

2 medium onions, chopped or
  2 cups TJ's Diced Onions

1 ¼ teaspoons TJ's Crushed
  Garlic or 4 cloves garlic, minced

2 cup lentils, uncooked, sorted
  and rinsed

½ cup brown rice, uncooked

2 (10-12 ounce) packages frozen
  chopped spinach, partially
  thawed and separated

3 vegetable bouillon cubes,
  crushed

4 cups water

½ cup chopped tomato, for
  garnish

2 tablespoons chopped mint,
  for garnish

Combine all ingredients except garnishes in a 3 ½-quart slow-cooker. Cover and cook on LOW 7 to 8 hours, or until rice and lentils are tender but not mushy. Garnish with tomato and mint.

Per serving: 305 calories, 1 g fat, 0 mg cholesterol, 646 mg sodium, 55 g carbohydrate, 13 g fiber, 20 g protein

Option:
Instead of tomato and mint, sprinkle vegetarian bacon bits over this dish before serving.

 Dairy-free

 Vegan

Butternut Squash and White Bean Soup

My husband found this recipe in a *Cooking Light* magazine years ago, and I adapted it to the slow cooker. It is one of our favorites.

Serves 6

2 (12 ounce) packages TJ's Cut Butternut Squash or 3 cups cubed butternut squash

1 medium onion, finely chopped; or 1 cup TJ's Diced Onions

¾ teaspoon cinnamon

½ teaspoon cumin

⅓ teaspoon TJ's Crushed Garlic or 1 clove garlic, minced

⅛ teaspoon ground black pepper

14 ounces TJ's Chicken Broth

1 (14 ½-ounce) can TJ's Diced Tomatoes, undrained

1 (14 ½ ounce) can TJ's Diced & Fire Roasted Tomatoes with Green Chiles, undrained

1 (15 ounce) can cannellini beans or Northern white beans, rinsed and drained

Combine all ingredients in a 3½- to 5-quart slow cooker. Cover and cook on LOW for 6 to 8 hours.

Per serving: 245 calories, 0.6 g fat, 0 mg cholesterol, 600 mg sodium, 22 g carbohydrate, 8.5 g fiber, 4.6 g protein

Options:

- For a vegetarian version, substitute dry chicken-flavored vegetarian powder and 14 ounces water, or use vegetable broth.
- Substitute 1 (14 ounce) can Mexican-style stewed tomatoes for TJ's Diced & Fire Roasted Tomatoes with Green Chiles.
- Add chicken or tofu to add protein.

 Dairy-free

 *Gluten-free if use TJ's Organic Free Range Chicken Broth or Organic Low Sodium Chicken Broth

Carne Asada Tacos

One of my clients had the idea of cooking this meat in the slow cooker while she and her husband were at work and added it to her family's regular menu rotation. It could also be used as a filling for burritos or served over rice and vegetables.

Serves 6

1 onion, chopped or 1 cup TJ's
   Diced Onions
1 (about 24 ounce) package
   TJ's Carne Asada
2 teaspoons extra virgin olive oil
1 (16 ounce) package
   Mélange à Trois
12 corn tortillas
Chopped lettuce
Low-fat cheese, optional
Sliced avocado, optional

1. Place onion in the bottom of a 3 ½ -quart slow cooker; add Carne Asada and cook on LOW 6 to 8 hours, or until a meat thermometer inserted into the meat reads 160ºF.
2. In a nonstick skillet over medium-high heat, cook bell peppers about 3 minutes, stirring frequently.
3. Heat tortillas and place meat, onions, peppers, lettuce and cheese and avocado, if desired, onto the tortillas.

Per Serving (2 tacos): *(based on 24 ounce package of meat) 339 calories, 11 g fat, 60 mg cholesterol, 479 mg sodium, 31 g carbohydrate, 5.6 g fiber, 27.6 g protein*

 Dairy-free without optional cheese

Chapter 15:

Simple Desserts

Yes, you can have dessert when you are living lean, especially if it is light and delicious like the ones in this chapter. You will find mostly fruit-based recipes with very little, if any, additional sugar added and, like the rest of the recipes in this book, void of artificial ingredients, including artificial sweeteners.

Portion size is important to take into account when eating anything, but especially dessert, so if you are budgeting your calories pay attention to the recipe serving size. Savor each bite and enjoy it, guilt-free.

Weight Watcher Points™ are available online at my website: www.HealthyTraderJoes.com.

Chocolate Banana "Ice Cream"

Once you try this, you will want to make it again. Freeze several bananas while you are at it for the next time you are in the mood for chocolate ice cream but want to stay within your caloric and fat range. For each banana, I usually peel it, break it into 4 pieces and then place it in a freezer bag.

Serves 4

2 bananas, peeled and frozen for
at least 2 hours
2 teaspoons unsweetened cocoa

Take bananas out of the freezer and let them sit for about 10 minutes. Put bananas into a food processor and blend for about 1 ½ minutes, scraping often with a spatula. Add cocoa and process for several seconds until smooth.

Per serving (depending on the size of the bananas): *67 calories, 1 g fat, 0 mg cholesterol, 1 mg sodium, 17.25 g carbohydrate, 2.0 g fiber, 1 g protein*

Options:
- Add peanut butter before mixing or add Puffins Peanut Butter cereal as a topping.
- Use TJ's Pumpkin Butter in place of chocolate.
- Top with crushed vanilla wafers or low-fat granola.

If you're feeling decadent, make chocolate "syrup" by combining 2 tablespoons of TJ's Agave Nectar with 1 tablespoon cocoa powder.

 Gluten-free

 Vegan

Chocolate Banana Dessert

Chocolate Banana Dessert is similar to the previous recipe but doesn't taste like ice cream and can be made on impulse, as the banana is fresh.

Serves 1

1 tablespoon semisweet
chocolate chips
½ banana, thinly sliced
1 tablespoon nonfat vanilla
yogurt, or 1 tablespoon nonfat
Greek style yogurt mixed with
⅛ teaspoon vanilla and a dash
of stevia

Melt chocolate chips in a small bowl in the microwave. Top banana slices with the chocolate and yogurt.

Per serving: *117 calories, 3 g fat, 0 mg cholesterol, 14 mg sodium, 23 g carbohydrate, 2 g fiber, 2 g protein*

 Gluten-free

 Vegetarian

Strawberries Dipped in Honeyed Yogurt

Serve this at a party or gathering as finger-food. To serve as a dessert, place sliced strawberries in 4 bowls and top with yogurt-honey sauce.

Serves 4

1 cup nonfat plain Greek style yogurt
1 ½ tablespoons honey
20 strawberries with stems

In a medium bowl, mix yogurt and honey until well blended. Dip strawberries in yogurt.

Per serving (5 strawberries): 75 calories, 0 g fat, 0 mg cholesterol, 24 mg sodium, 7 g carbohydrate, 1.3 g fiber, 6 g protein

Options:
- Add 1 teaspoon vanilla extract.
- Use agave nectar in place of honey.

 Gluten-free

 Vegetarian

Cinnamon "Baked" Apple

This is a super-simple recipe you can enjoy in just minutes. For one serving, microwave the apple on high for 2 to 4 minutes.

Serves 4

4 Rome Beauty or Granny Smith
    apples (about 2 pounds), cored
    and peeled an inch down from
    the stem end
½ cup apple juice or
    2 tablespoons frozen apple
    juice concentrate, reconstituted
½ teaspoon ground cinnamon
Freshly grated nutmeg
2 tablespoons nonfat Greek style
    yogurt, low-fat vanilla ice cream
    or frozen yogurt, optional

1. Place apples in a 2-quart round, covered glass casserole dish.
2. Spoon apple juice over apples. Sprinkle with cinnamon and nutmeg.
3. Cover and bake in microwave on high for 9 to 11 minutes. They will be tender when pierced with a fork.
4. Spoon nonfat Greek yogurt, low-fat ice cream or frozen yogurt over the top, if desired.

Per serving: *90 calories, 0.5 g fat, 0 mg cholesterol, 0 mg sodium, 23 g carbohydrate, 3.0 g fiber, 0.5 g protein*

Options:
- Substitute orange juice or unsweetened papaya juice in place of apple juice.
- Substitute brandy or a combination of brandy and rum for half the fruit juice.
- Stuff the core of the apples with raisins, dates and walnuts before baking.

 *Dairy-free without optional yogurt, ice cream or frozen yogurt

 Gluten-free

 Vegetarian

Super-Simple Pumpkin Brown Rice Dessert

Pumpkin Butter is a blend of pumpkin, cinnamon, nutmeg, cloves and sugar. When it's added to rice and milk, it makes a tasty, very easy dessert.

Serves 2

½ pouch frozen TJ's Brown Rice or
   1 cup cooked brown rice
4 teaspoons TJ's Pumpkin Butter
   (seasonal)
½ cup low-fat milk or evaporated
   skim milk
4 tablespoons non- or low-fat
   vanilla yogurt, ice cream or
   Greek style yogurt, optional

Combine all the ingredients except the optional topping in a microwaveable bowl. Cover and heat for about 2 minutes. Stir, place in two bowls and add topping if desired.

Per serving: 133 calories, 1.1 g fat, 3.5 mg cholesterol, 32 mg sodium, 26 g carbohydrate, 1.5 g fiber, 4.5 g protein

Options:

- Substitute applesauce and cinnamon, nutmeg and cloves for pumpkin butter. Add stevia to sweeten, if desired.
- Substitute almond milk or rice milk in place of milk.
- Add a little low-fat cream cheese or Tofutti Better than Cream Cheese before heating.
- Sprinkle a teaspoon of ground flaxseeds over each serving to add fiber.
- For a creamier version, place in a food processor and blend for 10 seconds or until desired consistency.

 *Dairy-free if you use nut or soy milk and soy yogurt if adding topping

 Gluten-free

 Vegetarian

Grilled Pineapple with Mango Sorbet

This is a very simple yet elegant dessert that needs to be refrigerated for an hour before serving. The recipe is adapted from one in Dr. Shapiro's *Picture Perfect Weight Loss Cookbook.*

Serves 4

2 tablespoons TJ's Seasoned Rice Vinegar

2 tablespoons chopped fresh mint

1 tablespoon fresh lime juice

1 tablespoon brown sugar

1 teaspoon grated lime zest

1 teaspoon fresh grated ginger or ¾ teaspoon bottled minced ginger

1 (16 ounce) package TJ's fresh pineapple or use a fresh pineapple, cut into slices

1 cup TJ's Mango Sorbet

1. In a medium bowl, combine the vinegar, chopped mint, lime juice, brown sugar, lime peel and ginger.
2. Heat a heavy griddle over medium-high heat and spray with cooking spray.
3. Add the pineapple and cook for 5 minutes on each side, or until lightly browned.
4. Place the pineapple in a dish and top with the sauce. Cover and refrigerate for about an hour.
5. Divide the pineapple among 4 small plates and top each with ¼ cup mango sorbet.

Per serving: 127 calories, 0.5 g fat, 0 mg cholesterol, 122 mg sodium, 33 g carbohydrate, 1.3 g fiber, 0 g protein

 Vegan

Yogurt Parfait

When you taste this dessert, you might forget it's actually good for you!

Serves 4

2 cups nonfat Greek style yogurt
1 cup sliced strawberries
½ cup TJ's Low Fat Granola with
    Almonds or other low-fat
    granola
4 parfait glasses

In a parfait glass, layer Greek style
yogurt and sliced strawberries.
Sprinkle with low-fat granola.

Per serving: 102 calories, 0.67 g fat, 0 mg cholesterol, 47 mg sodium, 13 g carbohydrate, 1.7 g fiber, 12 g protein

 Vegetarian

Tropical Yogurt Dessert

This yogurt and fruit dessert adds a bit more pizzaz to your meal, along with 400 mg of calcium, or about 1/3 of the RDA for women, who need between 1,000 and 1,200 mg/day, depending on age. The recipe is adapted from the *Eat More, Weigh Less* cookbook.

Serves 4

1 ½ cups TJ's Nonfat Plain Yogurt

4 teaspoons agave nectar or honey

¼ teaspoon cinnamon

½ teaspoon pure vanilla extract

¼ teaspoon rum extract

1⅓ cups fresh TJ's Pineapple, diced or use frozen TJ's Pineapple Tidbits

¼ cup frozen TJ's Orange Juice Concentrate

1⅓ cups sliced bananas

⅔ cups sliced fresh strawberries or use frozen

⅔ cup fresh raspberries, or use frozen

4 teaspoons fresh mint, optional

1. Whisk together yogurt, honey, cinnamon and the two extracts in a medium-size bowl. Cover and refrigerate.
2. Combine pineapple and orange juice concentrate in a 2 ½-quart saucepan. Bring to a boil and reduce the heat to simmer. Simmer 5 to 7 minutes, stirring frequently. Cool.
3. Transfer cooled pineapple to a large bowl. Add the bananas and berries and toss to coat.
4. To serve, divide fruit into 4 bowls and spoon yogurt sauce over each. Garnish with mint.

Per serving: *171 calories, 1 g fat, 1.5 mg cholesterol, 60 mg sodium, 38 g carbohydrate, 3.8 g fiber, 6 g protein*

Option:
Use TJ's frozen Mango Chunks in place of berries.

 Gluten-free

 Vegetarian

Peach Pizza

While this dessert is neither super-sweet nor high in fat, it hits the spot when you want dessert but don't want to spend the next day regretting it. This dessert pizza could also be served as part of a brunch menu. The recipe is adapted from *Better Homes and Gardens Big Book of 30 Minute Dinners*.

Serves 8

Cooking spray

1 bag refrigerated TJ's Wheat Pizza Dough or prepared plain pizza crust

¼ cup packed brown sugar

3 tablespoons flour

3 tablespoons butter or margarine, melted

1 (25 ounce) jar TJ's Peach Halves, drained

½ cup quick-cooking rolled oats

1. Preheat oven to 400ºF.
2. Spray pizza pan with cooking spray and spread the pizza dough onto the pan.
3. Place the pan on the lowest rack of the oven and bake for 15 minutes, or until the pizza shell just begins to brown.
4. Slice peach halves in four even pieces and place on top of pizza shell.
5. Mix oats, brown sugar and flour together in a small bowl. Cut in butter or margarine until the mixture is coarse. Sprinkle the oat mixture over the peaches.
6. Bake on the top shelf of the oven for 12 to15 minutes, until the dough begins to brown. Slice into 8 slices with a pizza cutter. Serve warm or at room temperature.

Per serving: 262 calories, 6.7 g fat, 11 mg cholesterol, 243 mg sodium, 49 g carbohydrate, 3.2 g fiber, 7.4 g protein

Options:
- Use fresh peaches, pears, nectarines or berries.
- Use a combination of peaches and pineapple.

Vegetarian

Strawberry Pizza

This recipe has way less sugar, fat and calories than a traditional fruit tart. It reminds me of a breakfast pastry and could also be served for brunch.

Serves 8

Cooking spray
1 TJ's Wheat Pizza Dough or prepared plain pizza crust
1 tablespoon butter or margarine, melted
1 cup TJ's Fat Free Ricotta Cheese
8 ounces TJ's Light Cream Cheese, at room temperature
½ cup powdered sugar
1 teaspoon vanilla extract
2 cups sliced strawberries
½ teaspoon sugar mixed with ⅛ teaspoon cinnamon

1. Preheat oven to 400ºF.
2. Spray pizza pan with cooking spray and spread the pizza dough onto the pan.
3. Brush the butter or margarine over the crust and place the pan on the lowest rack of the oven; bake for 15 minutes, or until pizza shell just begins to brown. Let cool for a few minutes.
4. While pizza shell is baking, beat ricotta, cream cheese and powdered sugar with an electric hand mixer until fluffy.
5. Spread cream cheese mixture over the crust, leaving a 1-inch border around the edge. Bake 5 minutes. Cool completely.
6. Top pizza with sliced strawberries and sprinkle with cinnamon sugar. Slice with a pizza wheel.

Per serving: 263 calories, 7.6 g fat, 17 mg cholesterol, 582 mg sodium, 63 g carbohydrate, 3.3 g fiber, 9.8 g protein

Options:
- Use other fruit in place of strawberries.
- For a softer texture, bake only 10 minutes in step 3.
- Use TJ's Plain Pizza Dough in place of TJ's Wheat Pizza Dough.

 Vegetarian

Gingered Peach and/or Pear Crisp

This crisp tastes similar to a peach cobbler, but it has a ginger snap zip. It's super-easy to put together and only has 147 calories per serving. To crush cookies, place a cup of cookies in a durable plastic bag and roll a rolling pin over them. The recipe is adapted from one in *Better Homes and Gardens Big Book of 30 Minute Dinners*

Serves 6

1 (25 ounce) jar TJ's Peach Halves, drained and sliced
1 teaspoon grated fresh ginger or bottled minced ginger
½ cup finely crushed TJ's Triple Ginger Snaps (12 cookies)
½ cup quick-cooking oats
2 tablespoons brown sugar, unpacked

1. Preheat oven to 425ºF (or 400ºF if using a glass dish).
2. Place peaches and ginger in an 8-inch shallow pan and stir until ginger is blended in.
3. In a small bowl, stir together gingersnaps, oats and brown sugar. Sprinkle over fruit.
4. Bake 15 to 20 minutes, until browned.

Per serving: *147 calories, 2 g fat, 8.3 mg cholesterol, 52 mg sodium, 30 g carbohydrate, 1.5 g fiber, 2.5 g protein*

Option:
Substitute a combination of canned peach and pear halves, or use fresh fruit.

 *For a dairy-free version, substitute TJ's Cookie Thins Triple Ginger or TJ's Gluten Free Ginger Snaps

*For a gluten-free version, use TJ's Gluten Free Ginger Snaps and Bob's Red Mill Gluten-free Oatmeal or other certified gluten-free oatmeal

Vegetarian

Greek Yogurt, Lemon Curd and Ginger Snaps

Sometimes you want something sweet and you just want a tiny bit. This recipe is great for those times.

Serves 1

2 tablespoons nonfat Greek style
    yogurt
½ tablespoon TJ's Lemon Curd
Lemon zest, optional
5 TJ's Cookie Thins Triple Ginger
    cookies or other ginger cookies

Combine yogurt with lemon curd.
Spread onto cookies.

Per serving: 142 calories, 4 g fat, 20.5 mg cholesterol,
81 mg sodium, 22.8 g carbohydrate, 0 g fiber,
3.75 g protein

 *Gluten-free if you use TJ's Gluten Free Ginger
    Snaps in place of ginger cookies

 Vegetarian

Instant Berry Frozen Yogurt

Make your own frozen yogurt with this easy and delicious recipe. Serve it immediately.

Serves 4

1 cup plain nonfat yogurt
2 ½ tablespoons honey or
    agave nectar
½ teaspoon pure vanilla extract
¾ cup frozen strawberries
¾ cup frozen raspberries

1. Combine yogurt, honey and vanilla in a food
   processor and process until smooth.
2. With the processor running, drop in the frozen
   berries gradually, until the yogurt becomes
   smooth.
3. Serve immediately with a berry atop the yogurt
   for garnish.

Per serving: 72 calories, 0 g fat, 0 mg cholesterol,
40 mg sodium, 24 g carbohydrate, 2.5 g fiber,
3.6 g protein

 Gluten-free

 *For a vegan version, use plain soy yogurt in
    place of yogurt

Appendix

M	Daily Totals: 1372 calories, 31 g fat, 128 mg cholesterol, 1562 mg sodium, 189 g carbohydrate, 32 g fiber, 82 g protein				
Breakfast	**Snack 1**	**Lunch**	**Snack 2**	**Dinner**	
Yonola, 282 calories, page 195	2 Mini Babybel Light cheeses, 100 calories	Chicken Lime Burger, 285 calories, page 50 apple, 95 calories	½ package Just a Handful Almonds, 105 calories	Tropical Chicken and Rice, 320 calories, page 114 green salad with cooked vegetables, 50 calories 2 tablespoons Champagne Pear Vinaigrette, 45 calories 3 pineapple rings, 90 calories	

Tu	Daily Totals: 1304 calories, 40 g fat, 257 mg cholesterol, 1635 mg sodium, 150 g carbohydrate, 39 g fiber, 74 g protein				
Breakfast	**Snack 1**	**Lunch**	**Snack 2**	**Dinner**	
Breakfast Burrito, 257 calories, page 37	6 ounces low-fat plain yogurt with 8 strawberries, 130 calories	Hummus and Tuna Spread, 200 calories, page 52 1 cup of raw broccoli and cucumber, 25 calories 4 tablespoons TJ's Tzatziki, 60 calories banana, 100 calories	1 stalk celery with 1 tablespoon peanut butter, 110 calories	Grilled Eggplant Mélange and Cannellini Beans, 332 calories, page 144 Cooked green beans and mushrooms with 1 teaspoon olive oil, 90 calories	

W	Daily Totals: 1387 calories, 42 g fat, 147 mg cholesterol, 1927 mg sodium, 154 g carbohydrate, 22 g fiber, 79 g protein				
Breakfast	**Snack 1**	**Lunch**	**Snack 2**	**Dinner**	
Fruit Smoothie, 270 calories, page 86	Light Mini Babybel Cheese, 50 calories 3 Ak-Mak crackers, 70 calories	Asparagus Veggie Sandwich, 373 calories, page 60	1 cup TJ's Organic Low Sodium Tomato and Roasted Red Pepper Soup, 100 calories	Glazed Apricot Salmon, 385 calories, page 130 Spinach Salad with Peanut Vinaigrette, 102 calories, page 80 Broccoli with Lemon Zest, 38 calories, page 165	

Th	Daily Totals: 1362 calories, 31 g fat, 127 mg cholesterol, 1798 mg sodium, 188 g carbohydrate, 31 g fiber, 91 g protein				
Breakfast	**Snack 1**	**Lunch**	**Snack 2**	**Dinner**	
On-the-Go Protein Shake, 203 calories, page 38 1 large orange, 86 calories	1 glass 1% fat milk, 110 calories	TJ's Mango, Red Quinoa and Chicken Salad, 240 calories 1 TJ's Whole Wheat Tortilla, 101 calories	2 TJ's Turkey Meatballs with salsa or other sauce, 110 calories	Peanut-Tamarind Sweet Potato Curry, 320 calories, page 154 Broccoli Peanut Slaw, 90 calories, page 81 Yogurt Parfait, 102 calories, page 189	

F | *Daily Totals: 1437 calories, 22 g fat, 57 mg cholesterol, 1925 mg sodium, 194 g carbohydrate, 28 g fiber, 87 g protein*

Breakfast	Snack 1	Lunch	Snack 2	Dinner
Veggie Frittata Muffins, 168 calories, page 31 Whole wheat toast, 80 calories 1 ¼ cup fresh pineapple, 95 calories	1/3 cup low-fat cottage cheese mixed with cinnamon and 1/3 cup low-fat fruit yogurt, 119 calories	Turkey Meatball Soup, 300 calories, page 96	½ red bell pepper and 4 tablespoons Eggplant Hummus, 110 calories	Chicken à la King with Asparagus, 353 calories, page 106 Green Salad with Figs and Champagne Pear Vinaigrette, 122 calories, page 76 Cinnamon "Baked" Apple, 90 calories, page 186

Sa | *Daily Totals: 1277 calories, 31 g fat, 99 mg cholesterol, 2048 mg sodium, 128 g carbohydrate, 22 g fiber, 114 g protein*

Breakfast	Snack 1	Lunch	Snack 2	Dinner
Vegetable Omelet, 260 calories, page 30	1 glass 1% low fat milk, 110 calories	Salmon Stuffed Pitas, 263 calories, page 51	¼ package TJ's Baked Teriyaki Tofu with ½ cup snap peas, 100 calories	Spicy Thai Noodle Bowls, 454 calories, page 119 Broccoli Peanut Slaw, 90 calories, page 81

Su | *Daily Totals: 1388 calories, 20 g fat, 78 mg cholesterol, 1371 mg sodium, 200 g carbohydrate, 31 g fiber, 78 g protein*

Breakfast	Snack 1	Lunch	Snack 2	Dinner
Yoats, 255 calories, page 29 ½ orange, 45 calories	¼ package TJ's Baked Tofu Teriyaki Flavor with ½ cup snap peas, 100 calories	TJ's Grilled Chicken Pasta Salad with Mango, 389 calories	½ package TJ's Just a Handful of Almonds, 105 calories	Mexican Chicken Stew, 294 calories, pages 112 to 113 1 cup frozen TJ's Brown Rice, 160 calories Spinach salad with TJ's Cilantro Salad Dressing, 55 calories

Grocery List for Week 1 Menu

The Week 1 menu provides a lot of variety. If you rotate between a couple of breakfasts during the week, you might want to modify these menus and shopping lists to accommodate those choices. I have tried to make those options easier by designating grocery items bought exclusively for breakfast with one asterisk, so that you can know which items to exclude from the shopping list.

All the following products are available at Trader Joe's, with the exception of some on the staples list, which are designated below. All are Trader Joe's label, unless designated otherwise. The items are listed by product groupings.

Salad Dressings

- 1 bottle Champagne Pear Vinaigrette
- 1 bottle Asian Style Spicy Peanut Vinaigrette
- 1 bottle Cilantro Salad Dressing

Vegetables

- 2 bags salad greens
- 2 bags fresh spinach
- 3 bags fresh broccoli florets, or buy frozen
- 1 bag sugar snap peas
- 2 small zucchini
- 1 package crimini or white mushrooms
- 1 package shredded carrots
- 1 package shredded cabbage
- 1 package broccoli slaw
- 1 package endive
- 2 English cucumbers
- 1 bunch celery
- 2 bunches green onions
- 3 red bell peppers
- 1 package green beans or buy frozen
- 2 tomatoes
- 1 package Sweet Potato Spears or 1 pound sweet potatoes
- parsley, optional
- cilantro, optional
- basil
- 3 yellow onions
- 1 red onion
- 2 limes
- 1 package fresh jalapeño, or buy canned
- 1 package fresh ginger, or use bottled minced ginger (not available at Trader Joe's)

Fruit

- apples (need 1 per person)
- 1 large orange
- 1 package fresh pineapple
- *2 baskets of strawberries, (1 basket each for breakfast and dessert)
- *4 bananas (2 are for breakfast)

Refrigerated Salads, Cheese, Chicken and More

- 1 TJ's Red Quinoa and Chicken Salad
- 1 package Mini Babybel Light Cheese (besides snacks, use for recipes calling for light cheese)
- *1 small wedge Parmigianino Reggiano or Parmesan cheese
- *shredded low fat cheddar (2 tablespoons)
- 1 package light Swiss cheese
- 2 packages Just Chicken
- 1 container Spicy Hummus
- 1 container Eggplant Hummus
- 1 package guacamole or an avocado
- 1 carton Tzatziki (or use yogurt for this snack)
- 1 package Baked Teriyaki Tofu

Dairy and Eggs

- 1 small carton Light Sour Cream (just need ¼ cup, could use yogurt instead for Salmon Stuffed Pitas if you do not need sour cream for foods outside of plan)
- *1 (32 ounce) carton skim or low-fat yogurt (most of this is for breakfasts)
- 1 (16 ounce) carton nonfat Greek style yogurt
- *2 (16 ounce) cartons egg whites, or 1 larger carton, or 2 dozen eggs
- *1 (32 ounce) carton low- or nonfat milk (1 1/3 cups is for breakfasts)

Breads and Cereals

- 1 package corn tortillas
- 1 package whole wheat hamburger buns
- 1 loaf whole wheat bread
- 1 Focaccia loaf
- 1 package whole wheat pita pockets
- *1 box low-fat granola
- *1 package regular (not instant) oatmeal

Grocery

- 1 jar almond butter or refrigerated container of Tahini Sauce
- 1 jar Organic Reduced Sugar Apricot Preserves
- 1 can albacore tuna in water
- 1 (14.75 ounce) can salmon
- 2 cans black beans
- 1 can cannellini beans
- 1 packet Taco Mix
- 1 can Fire Roasted Chiles
- 1 package wild rice
- 1 carton Low Sodium Chicken Broth
- 1 carton Low Sodium Vegetable Broth (unless you want to use chicken broth in the vegetarian dishes)
- 1 carton Organic Low Sodium Tomato and Roasted Red Pepper Soup
- 2 cans Diced & No Salt Added Tomatoes
- olive oil spray
- 1 bottle Sesame Soy Ginger Vinaigrette
- 1 bag Whole Wheat Rotelle
- 1 bottle 21 Seasoning Salute
- 1 jar tomato salsa or refrigerated container of fresh salsa
- *1 container unsweetened almond milk (can use regular milk if not vegan or dairy-free)
- *1 can or container of protein powder
- 1 package Just a Handful of Almonds

Frozen

- 1 package Turkey Meatballs
- 1 box Chile Lime Burgers
- 1 package Just Grilled Chicken Strips
- 2 packages asparagus spears
- 1 package Grilled Eggplant and Zucchini Mélange
- 1 package Mélange à Trios
- 1 package Fire Roasted Bell Peppers and Onions
- *1 package frozen mixed vegetables (your choice)
- 1 package corn
- 2 boxes brown rice, organic or otherwise
- 1 package cooked medium shrimp, tails off
- 2 pounds wild Silverbrite salmon or other salmon
- frozen orange juice concentrate (or fresh orange juice – you will need 1 ½ cups for recipes)
- *1 package frozen blueberries, or use fresh
- 1 package Pineapple Tidbits, or purchase fresh or canned

Menu ingredients not available at Trader Joe's

- 8 ounces thin rice noodles
- tamarind paste (or use lime as substitute)

Staples available at Trader Joe's

- reduced fat mayonnaise
- natural style peanut butter
- brown sugar
- curry powder
- dried thyme
- white flour
- 12 ounce can evaporated skim milk, available seasonal only
- sesame seeds, optional
- crushed garlic
- extra virgin olive oil
- chopped peanuts (1/4 cup)
- cornstarch

Staples not available at Trader Joe's

- cardamom
- dried dill
- bacon bits, optional

M	Daily Totals: 1324 calories, 29 g fat, 117 mg cholesterol, 1428 mg sodium, 173 g carbohydrate, 32 g fiber, 77 g protein				
Breakfast	**Snack 1**	**Lunch**	**Snack 2**	**Dinner**	
Veggie Frittata Muffins, 168 calories, page 31 whole wheat toast, 86 calories 1 small orange, 43 calories	1 large red bell pepper or other vegetables, 30 calories 4 tablespoons TJ's Eggplant Hummus, 70 calories	Ginger Tuna Rice Salad, 226 calories 20 baby carrots, 60 calories	1/2 package Just a Handful of Almonds, 105 calories	Awesome Turkey Chili, 280 calories, page 178 Carrot and Beet Salad with Arugula, 46 calories, page 77 2 corn tortillas, 120 calories Cinnamon "Baked" Apple, 90 calories, page 186	

Tu	Daily Totals: 1352 calories, 36 g fat, 180 mg cholesterol, 2019 mg sodium, 155 g carbohydrate, 34.1 g fiber, 72 g protein				
Breakfast	**Snack 1**	**Lunch**	**Snack 2**	**Dinner**	
1 ½ servings Ricotta-Peanut Butter Breakfast Spread, 150 calories, page 32 Whole wheat toast, 86 calories, ½ cup blueberries, 40 calories	1 bag TJ's 94% Fat Free Microwave Popcorn, 130 calories	Burrito for One, 282 calories, page 146 ¼ avocado, 72 calories 10 baby carrots, 50 calories	½ cup plain low-fat yogurt, 77 calories 8 medium strawberries, 28 calories	Carrot and Beet Salad with Arugula, 46 calories, page 77 Broiled Shrimp with Papaya Mango Salsa, 352 calories, page 134 Lemony Asparagus with Parsley, 45 calories, page 164	

W	Daily Totals: 1420 calories, 39 g fat, 95 mg cholesterol, 1226 mg sodium, 245 g carbohydrate, 31 g fiber, 72 g protein				
Breakfast	**Snack 1**	**Lunch**	**Snack 2**	**Dinner**	
On-the-Go Protein Shake, 203 calories, page 38	½ package Just a Handful of Almonds, 105 calories	Frozen TJ's Thai Style Massaman Chicken (serves 1) 390 calories 1 large stalk of celery, 10 calories, spread with 1 tablespoon of chunky peanut butter, 94 calories	½ large apple, 62 calories, with 1 Light Baby Minibel cheese, 50 calories	Tzatziki Soup, 145 calories, page 100 Lentil Pasta, 361 calories, page 161	

Th Daily Totals: 1383 calories, 34 g fat, 128 mg cholesterol, 2393 mg sodium, 165 g carbohydrate, 35 g fiber, 84 g protein

Breakfast	Snack 1	Lunch	Snack 2	Dinner
Veggie Burger Breakfast Sandwich, 234 calories, page 34 1 cup 1% fat milk, 110 calories	1 large red bell pepper or other vegetables, 30 calories dipped in 4 tablespoons Eggplant Hummus, 70 calories	Tuna and Marinated Bean Salad with Bruschetta, 197 calories, page 55 1 banana, 100 calories	½ cup fat free ricotta cheese, 90 calories (use plain yogurt if did not purchase ricotta) 8 large strawberries, 45 calories, optional: add a dash of honey or agave and balsamic	Low Sodium Tomato and Roasted Red Pepper Soup, 100 calories Ranch "Fried" Chicken, 207 calories, page 122 Quinoa Duo with Vegetable Mélange, 220 calories TJ's Beans So Green, 90 calories

F Daily Totals: 1396 calories, 46 g fat, 189 mg cholesterol, 2,073 mg sodium, 171 g carbohydrates, 31 g fiber, 94 g protein

Breakfast	Snack 1	Lunch	Snack 2	Dinner
Tofu Scramble, 117 calories, page 40 TJ's Country Potatoes with Haricot Verts and Wild Mushrooms, 130 calories ½ cup pineapple, 38 calories	½ cup TJ's O's cereal, 55 calories ½ cup 1% fat milk, 50 calories	2 servings Broccoli Peanut Slaw, 180 calories, page 81 3 ounces cooked shrimp, 80 calories 3/4 cup cooked brown rice, 120 calories	1 1/3 cup sugar snap peas, 70 calories 4 tablespoons TJ's Tzatziki, 60 calories	Awesome Turkey Chili, 280 calories, page 178 3 cups fresh spinach or salad, 20 calories 1 medium tomato, 25 calories 2 tablespoons TJ's Cilantro Salad Dressing, 50 calories 2 corn tortillas, 120 calories

Sa Daily Totals: 1398 calories, 41 g fat, 30 mg cholesterol, 2085 mg sodium, 195 g carbohydrates, 35 g fiber, 63 g protein

Breakfast	Snack 1	Lunch	Snack 2	Dinner
Yonola, 282 calories, page 29	1 red bell pepper 4 tablespoons TJ's Eggplant Hummus, 110 calories	Frozen TJ's Reduced Guilt Mac and Cheese (serves 1), 270 calories 1 1/3 cup sugar snap peas, 70 calories, 4 tablespoons TJ's Tzatziki, 60 calories	½ package Just a Handful of Almonds, 105 calories	Butternut Squash Peanut Butter Soup, 137 calories, page 95 Peanut Curry Tofu, 234 calories, page 143 2 servings of frozen Harvest Hodgepodge, steamed or microwaved, 60 calories 2 tablespoons Asian Style Spicy Peanut Vinaigrette, 70 calories

Breakfast	Snack 1	Lunch	Snack 2	Dinner
Yoats, 255 calories, page 29 1 small orange, 45 calories	1 Light Mini Babybel, 50 calories 2.5 Ak mak, 58 calories	Chicken Sandwich with Secret Sauce, 320 calories 3 cups fresh spinach, 20 calories 2 tablespoons TJ's Cilantro Salad Dressing, 45 calories	1 TJ's Turkey Meatball, 50 calories ½ TJ's Whole Wheat Pita Pocket, 50 calories 1 tablespoon TJ's Ttzatziki, 15 calories lettuce or cabbage, 5 calories	Seared Chili-Flavored Tuna, 120 calories, page 138 Amazing Watermelon Salad, 157 calories, page 84 Kale and Quinoa Pilaf, 218 calories, page 169

Grocery List for Week 2 Menu

As in the Week 1 menu, the Week 2 menu provides a lot of variety. If you rotate between a couple of breakfasts during the week, you might want to modify these menus and shopping lists to accommodate those choices. I have tried to make those options easier by designating grocery items bought exclusively for breakfast with one asterisk, so that you can know which items to exclude from the shopping list.

All the following products are available at Trader Joe's, with the exception of some on the staples list, which are designated below. All are Trader Joe's label, unless designated otherwise. The items are listed by product groupings. Review this grocery list if you used the menu from week 1 and cross off any items you already have.

Refrigerated

- 1 bottle Asian Style Spicy Peanut Vinaigrette
- 1 bottle Cilantro Salad Dressing
- 1 bottle Parmesan Ranch Dressing

Vegetables

- 2 bags fresh spinach, buy 1 more bag if feeding more than 2 people
- 1 package arugula
- 1 package kale
- 1 package cooked baby beets
- 1 package cut and peeled carrots
- 1 package sugar snap peas
- 1 package shredded carrots
- 1 package broccoli slaw
- 1 bunch celery
- 3 red bell peppers
- *3 tomatoes (one for breakfast)
- 2 bunches green onions
- 2 large onions and 1 medium onion or 3 bags diced onions
- 1 red onion
- fresh basil
- fresh mint, optional for watermelon salad
- fresh parsley, optional
- cilantro
- ginger (or use bottled ginger - which is not available at Trader Joe's)
- 1 sweet potato

Fruit

- *2 small oranges
- 2 oranges
- 3 lemons
- 1 lime
- 2 baskets of strawberries
- 2 packages sliced watermelon or 1 watermelon to serve four for salad
- 1 banana for lunch
- Apples - 2 per person for desserts
- Fresh ginger

Salads, Cheese, Chicken and more

- *1 (14 ounce) package Organic Firm Tofu for 4 servings
- 1 (14 ounce) package Organic Firm Tofu- need only 5 ounces for Peanut Curry Tofu so may need to buy only 1 package if making less servings of breakfast with tofu
- *1 carton fat-free ricotta for breakfast and snack
- 1 package crumbled feta cheese (need 1 cup)
- 1 package Mini Babybel Light Cheese
- 1 package steamed lentils
- 1 small wedge Parmigianino Reggiano or Parmesan cheese
- 1 container Eggplant Hummus
- 1 avocado
- 2 cartons Tzatziki - if serving fewer than 4 servings of soup for dinner, buy only 1 carton
- 1 carton Papaya Mango Salsa
- 2 pounds lean ground turkey or chicken
- 1 pound boneless skinless chicken breast halves

Dairy and Eggs

- *1 (32 ounce) container non - or low-fat plain yogurt (need 2 ¼ cups - most of this is for breakfasts but ½ cup is used for snack)
- *2 eggs
- *1 (32 ounce) carton skim or 1% fat milk - need 2 ½ cups for breakfast and 1 cup for snack
- 1 carton low fat buttermilk (for Tzatziki soup)
- *If you have not previously made Veggie Frittata Muffins (from week 1) and frozen them you will need:
- 1 (16 ounce) container egg whites or 8 egg whites plus 1 egg
- 1/3 cup skim milk
- ½ cup spinach
- ½ cup broccoli, diced
- ½ zucchini
- 4 mushrooms
- basil

Grocery

- 1 jar Reduced Sugar Apricot Spread
- 1 can sliced black olives
- 2 cans albacore tuna in water
- 2 cans black beans
- 1 can cannellini beans
- 1 can Refried Beans with Jalapeño Peppers
- 1 carton Low Sodium Chicken Broth
- 1 carton Low Sodium Tomato and Roasted Red Pepper Soup
- 2 cartons Butternut Squash Soup (to serve 4)
- 1 jar Curry Simmer Sauce
- 2 cans Diced & No Salt Added Tomatoes
- 2 cans kidney or pinto beans
- 1 box quinoa
- olive oil spray
- 1 bottle Fat Free Balsamic Vinaigrette
- 1 bottle Sesame Soy Ginger Vinaigrette
- 1 bag Whole Wheat Rotelle
- 1 box Garlic Mashed Potatoes
- 1 jar Bruschetta - or buy refrigerated container
- 1 bottle 21 Seasoning Salute
- *1 can or container of protein powder
- 1 package Just a Handful of Almonds
- 1 package 94% Fat-Free Microwave Popcorn
- 1 bottle Smoky, Spicy, Peach Salsa - or use left -over Papaya Mango Salsa
- 1 bottle Corn and Chile Tomato-Less Salsa
- 1 (12 ounce) bottle dark beer

Breads and Cereals

- 1 box low-fat granola
- *1 box regular oatmeal (not instant)
- 1 box O's (for snack)
- 1 package whole wheat hamburger buns
- 1 box Ak Mak crackers
- 1-2 packages corn tortillas - 1 person will need 4/week
- 1 package English Muffin Whole Wheat
- 1 loaf whole wheat bread
- 1 package whole wheat pita pockets
- 1 package whole wheat tortillas-or use corn tortillas

Frozen

- 1-2 packages frozen ahi tuna steaks (4 ounces/person)
- 1 package Dr. Praeger's California Veggie Burgers
- 1 package Turkey Meatballs
- 1 package Just Grilled Chicken Strips
- 1-2 packages Fire Roasted Vegetables with Balsamic Butter Sauce (2 servings/person)
- *1 package TJ's Country Potatoes with Haricot Verts and Wild Mushrooms
- 1 package Quinoa Duo with Vegetable Mélange
- 1 package asparagus spears
- 1 package Beans So Green
- 1 bowl Thai Style Massaman Chicken
- 1 box Reduced Guilt Mac and Cheese
- 1 package frozen peas
- 1-2 packages Hodgepodge (2 servings/person)
- 2 boxes organic brown rice
- 1 package cooked medium shrimp, tail off
- 1 package raw shrimp
- 1 package frozen blueberries or use fresh
- 1 package Pineapple Tidbits, or purchase fresh or canned

Staples Available at Trader Joe's

- Natural style peanut butter - 3 tablespoons needed
- balsamic vinegar
- 1 bay leaf
- ground cinnamon
- cayenne powder
- chili powder (1/4 cup)
- ground cumin
- dried oregano
- curry powder
- nutmeg
- paprika
- unsweetened cocoa powder
- turmeric
- honey
- pepper
- sea salt
- crushed garlic
- extra virgin olive oil
- reduced sodium soy sauce
- vanilla extract
- chopped peanuts (1/4 cup), optional item

Staples Not Available at Trader Joe's

- almond extract
- crushed red pepper flakes
- dried dill
- garam masala

If you find that you need more than 1400 calories per day according to the calculation on page 22, or if you are losing more than one percent of your body weight per week, use the ideas below to increase your calories to 1600 or 1800 per day.

For menus with 1600 calories, follow the above menus, but add 200 more calories per day by doubling the size of the snacks each day, adding an extra side to dinner, or adding a piece of fruit with lunch and dinner, depending on your dietary needs or health concerns.

For menus with 1800 calories, add 400 calories per day by doubling the snack size, choosing higher calorie meals from the cookbook, increasing meal portion size by about one third, adding sides to dinner and lunch, or by adding an occasional dessert from the cookbook, depending on your dietary needs or health concerns.

Index

Vegetarian Recipes

Dairy-free

The recipes listed in "Dairy-free" index do not contain dairy according to ingredients listed on their packages. Does not necessarily pertain to optional items listed in recipes or options listed along with recipes.

Gluten-free

The items listed do not contain gluten according to Trader Joe's ® "No Gluten Ingredients Used" list. Does not necessarily pertain to optional items listed in recipes or options listed along with recipes.

Acknowledgements

Writing a cookbook (as any book) is a phenomenal feat and many people help make it successful. I'd like to give special thanks to all those whose help and talents made this book possible:

My husband, Rich, for tasting almost every recipe and for supporting my efforts with this book as well as my other cookbooks and endeavors. Ross, my son, for providing honest critiques of the recipes and great suggestions for improvements. My son, Joel, for gracefully accepting that a corner of his room became my office while he was away at school.

Emily Callahan for emailing me about her successful weight loss using my *Quick and Healthy Meals from Trader Joe's* cookbook thus providing inspiration (along with my clients) for my writing *Livin' Lean with Trader Joe's*. At the time this book went to print she had lost 106.6 pounds! AWESOME! Way to go Emily!!

My weight management clients for allowing me to be part of their weight loss and life-changing journey. I am honored.

Tracy Taylor, R.D. for her excitement and enthusiasm for this project but mostly for her dedication to teaching her clients and others how to make eating healthfully convenient and delicious. She is a wonder.

Julie Motz for ongoing support and enthusiasm and for asking one good question that changed the direction of this book.

Wona Miniati and Deana Gunn for helping me to take this project beyond an intention; for helping Trader Joe's fans across the nation eat more creatively and for thinking BIG.

Carole Bidnick for sharing her expertise as well as her vision for this book; it kept me on track.

Dianne Jacob for editing and smoothing out my writing while helping to make my recipes more clear and concise.

Mitch Allen for freely sharing his professional expertise in publishing.

Cynthia Leslie-Bole for her help and insight throughout the process, for her enthusiasm and support for this book and for editing and proofreading.

Heather Smith for designing and creating a home for all of the recipes, lists, and menus.

Niels Glaser, for his support and printing expertise.

Trader Joe's for supplying healthy, creative and delicious products that can be quickly and conveniently transformed into tasty meals (with a little help) as well as for their helpful and friendly staff.

I am grateful to those who have generously shared their healthy recipes and renditions through cookbooks, online recipe sites, email, etc.; to members of East Bay Coaches, my cooking class students, members of the health and wellness collaborative of which I am a member, members of my book group, to those who have used my previous cookbooks and have let me know that you love them and found them helpful; to family, friends and neighbors who tasted many of the recipes and provided feedback and their enthusiasm for this book; and to all those who supported me with your best wishes for success.